United States
Department of
Agriculture

Forest Service

Southern
Research Station

General Technical
Report SRS–130

Past and Present Aquatic Habitats and Fish Populations of the Yazoo-Mississippi Delta

M.D. Bryant

The Author:

M.D. Bryant, Research Fishery Biologist, U.S. Department of Agriculture
Forest Service, Southern Research Station, Center for Bottomland Hardwood
Research, Stoneville, MS 38776.

Cover: Ten-mile Bayou, Delta National Forest, with large wood and riparian
trees on bank and in the channel.

November 2010

Southern Research Station
200 W.T. Weaver Blvd.
Asheville, NC 28804

Past and Present Aquatic Habitats and Fish Populations of the Yazoo-Mississippi Delta

M.D. Bryant

Past and Present Aquatic Habitats and Fish Populations of the Yazoo-Mississippi Delta

M.D. Bryant

Abstract

The goal of this review and synthesis of the literature, published and unpublished, is to describe the major processes that shape and influence the aquatic habitats and fish communities in the Yazoo-Mississippi Delta (YMD) and to outline a program of research. The YMD is influenced by the large geographic and temporal scales of the Mississippi River watershed. It extends over 41 percent of the contiguous United States. The Mississippi River has existed in its current location for more than 1.2 million years, and ancient fish species are still present in the watershed. About 9,500 years BP, the Mississippi River formed into a predominantly meandering channel from which most of the aquatic habitats in the YMD developed. Oxbows formed in the meander belts shape the topography of the YMD and are a fundamental part of the development of the aquatic habitat of the YMD. Seasonal floods are keystone events in the YMD, but the process is altered substantially from its previous natural state. Levees, flood control structures, land use practices, and loss of large wood in river channels have modified natural processes throughout most of the YMD. However, most of the larger fish species present during aboriginal occupation of the YMD are still present. Given the large-scale loss of habitat throughout the YMD and the deterioration of water quality, the abundance and diversity of fish likely have declined. In the past few years, management of aquatic habitats in the YMD has centered on mitigating and preventing some of the adverse effects of anthropogenic disturbance. A program of "naturalization" to move aquatic ecosystem processes closer to natural conditions is possible within the context of socioeconomic constraints. The research approach proposed in this paper provides a model to develop an understanding of the fish and aquatic habitat that can contribute to a sustainable restoration program.

Keywords: Aquatic habitat, bottomland hardwood forests, fish diversity, floodplain processes, floods, Mississippi River, Yazoo-Mississippi Alluvial Floodplain, Yazoo River.

> "THE RIVER HAD GONE, THREE MILES AWAY, BEYOND SIGHT AND SMELL, BEYOND THE DENSE TREES. IT CAME BACK ONLY IN FLOOD AND BOATS RAN OVER THE HOUSES."
>
> EUDORA WELTY: AT THE LANDING[1]

[1]Welty, Eudora The collected stories of Eudora Welty 1980 Harcourt Brace Joanvich

Introduction

The Mississippi River watershed is large and diverse, draining more than 3×10^6 km^2 (fig. 1). The Mississippi River and its tributaries, which include the Missouri and Ohio Rivers, constitute about 41 percent of the contiguous United States. It is the third largest river in the world (Baker and others 1991, Biedenharn and others 2000). The combined length of the Mississippi and Missouri Rivers is 6,211 km. The Missouri River and its tributaries descend from 4,200 m above sea level in the Rocky Mountains to the west. The Ohio River watershed includes the industrial and agricultural lands to the east. The watershed encompasses nine physiographic provinces, which include the Great Plains, the Appalachian Mountains, and the Gulf Coastal Plain (Robison 1986). The Lower Mississippi Alluvial Valley (LMAV) is located in the latter province.

Discharge—more than 475×10^8 m^3 of water per year—and sediment are dominant, naturally occurring geomorphic forces shaping habitats downstream. Human activity is the other major force and is directed at controlling the effects of discharge and sediment. The effects of these forces on downstream habitats are magnified by the large area of the watershed and by time scales that range from millennia to seasons. Seasonal floods shape habitats over the short term, but their cumulative effects are measured over centuries or more. The flood plain of the LMAV is the product of geologic evolution occurring over millennia.

The focus of this paper is the major processes that shape and influence the aquatic habitat and the fish communities in the Yazoo-Mississippi Delta (YMD). The four major goals of the paper are: (1) to provide a qualitative description of how major aquatic habitats and fish populations in the YMD evolved from geological and climatic conditions of the past; (2) to describe these processes before major anthropogenic alterations in the YMD; (3) to synthesize information on the hydrologic processes, existing landscape and aquatic habitats, and fish species communities in the YMD; and 4)

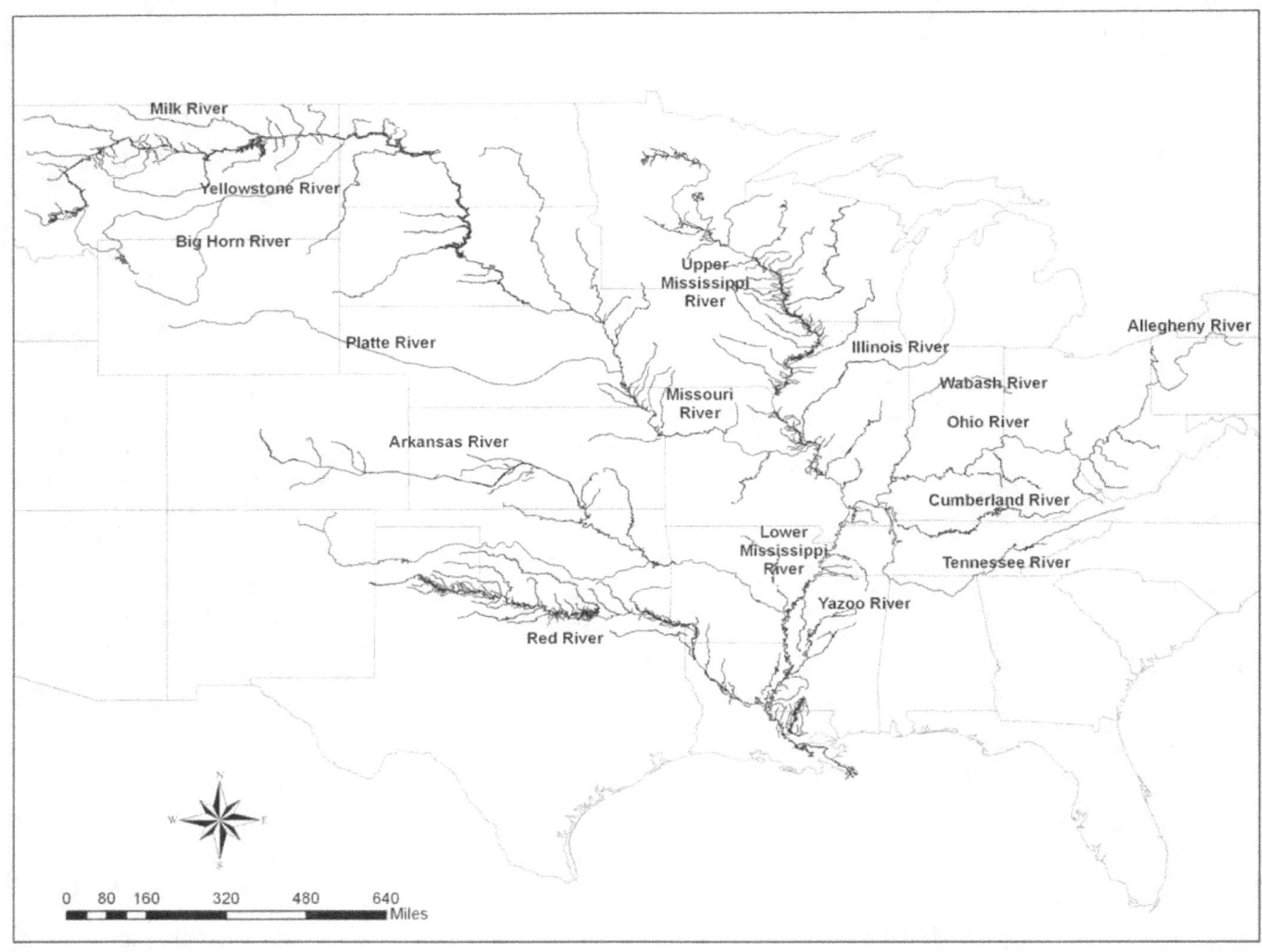

Figure 1—Mississippi River watershed and tributaries.

to use this information to propose a template for research to provide a scientific baseline for the management and restoration of aquatic habitats in the YMD. Information from past and existing conditions is important to identify information needs that will contribute to the improvement of aquatic habitats and processes that support fish populations.

Description of the Area

The YMD is a subregion of the LMAV. Saikku (2005) defines the YMD as the oval flood plain from the Mississippi River on the west with the eastern boundary on the bluffs from Memphis, TN, to Greenwood, MS, along the Yazoo River to Vicksburg, MS (fig. 2). The total area is 17,800 km². Major drainages within this area include the Yazoo River, fed by the Tallahatchie and Yalobusha Rivers on the

eastern boundary (Fisk 1944). Between the Mississippi and Yazoo Rivers are the Big Sunflower River, Deer Creek, and Steele Bayou. The Coldwater, Little Tallahatchie, Yocona, and Yalobusha Rivers feed the YMD from the uplands to the east. The first three drain into the Tallahatchie River, which is part of the Yazoo River drainage. The confluence of the Tallahatchie and Yalobusha Rivers forms the Yazoo River. The upland rivers are controlled by dams that form Arkabutla, Sardis, Enid, and Grenada lakes, respectively, all located along the bluff line hills along the eastern border of the YMD. Before construction of the mainline levees along the Mississippi River, the YMD was part of that river's flood plain and was historically prone to seasonal flooding (Fisk 1944, Barry 1998). Although the YMD is the area of interest for this paper, the YMD is influenced by a much larger geographic and longer temporal scale.

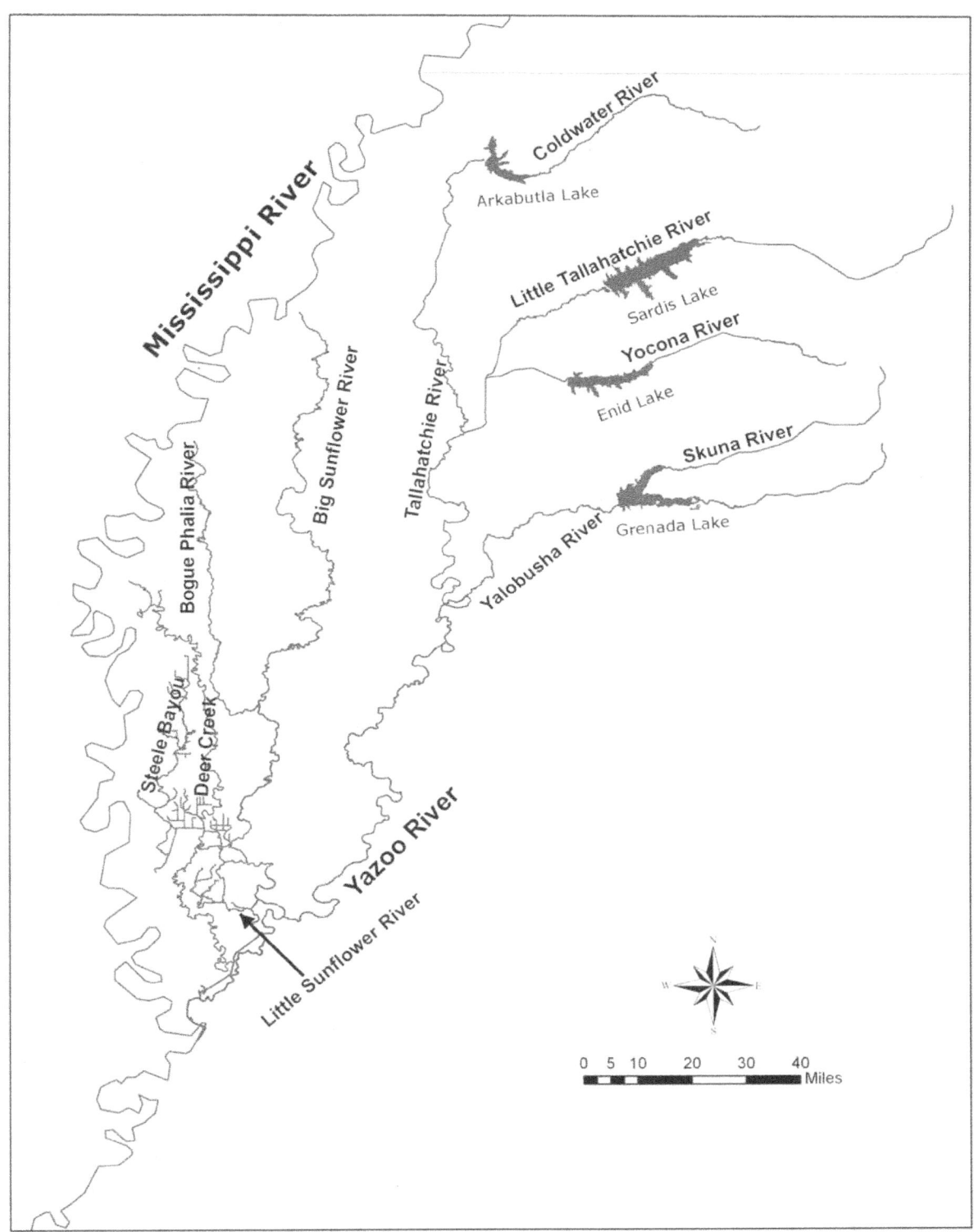

Figure 2—The Yazoo-Mississippi Delta flood plain and major drainages.

Geological History

The diverse ichthyofauna of the Mississippi River drainage is largely the result of the river's geological evolution. The Mississippi River apparently originated 50 to 60 million years BP by the end of the Cretaceous period after the formation of the North American continent (Robison 1986, Baker and others 1991). Over this period, its course and size varied with the major geological events that shaped the North American continent. Throughout the Tertiary, continental shallow inland seas formed and receded. By the early Pleistocene, major mountain ranges formed. By the late Tertiary, four large drainage basins formed that contributed to the present-day Mississippi drainage (Robison 1986). The upper and middle sections of the Missouri River flowed northward into the Hudson Bay drainage. The Great Plains drainage captured many of the rivers from the west, such as the Platte River and the Red River, and flowed southward into the Gulf of Mexico. The Laurentian System flowed through the Great Lakes and included rivers from the northeast, including the upper Ohio River. The Teays-Mississippi drainage occupied a drainage that is roughly analogous to the present-day location of the middle and lower Mississippi River. The Teays River drained much of what is now the Ohio River drainage. It connected to the Mississippi River in Illinois. The preglacial Mississippi River flowed through central and southern Illinois. The two drainages were separate until Pleistocene glaciation, which, among other things, forced fish into southern drainages. The Teays basin provided a refuge and reservoir for dispersal of fish (Robison 1986).

The present size of the Mississippi River likely formed about 1.5 to 2.2 million years BP as a result of advancing Midwestern glaciers that forced continental waters southward on the approximate present course of the river (Robison 1986, Baker and others 1991). The channel morphology in the Mississippi River drainage alternated between braided and meandering channel forms as a result of increasing and decreasing sediment loads from glacial advances and retreats (Autin and others 1991). Changes in sediment regimes generated by glaciation created a pattern of channel braiding and meandering that alternated over thousands of years. This pattern, accompanied by rising sea level and increased deposition of sediment, formed the flood plain in the present LMAV. With decreasing meltwater and sediment load, the river evolved into a predominantly meandering channel between 8,000 and 12,000 years BP. During the present meandering phase, oxbows, cutoffs, sloughs, and side channels developed, filled in, or were overrun as the river moved across the extensive flood plain and formed the topography of the YMD.

Although the morphology of the Mississippi River basin has undergone extensive change throughout its geological history, fish species representing many of the families present more than 5 million years BP still reside in the basin (Baker and others 1991). Few known extinctions of other species have occurred (Briggs 1986, Smith 1981). During this period, new species radiated into the diverse habitats as the Mississippi watershed responded to glacial expansions and contractions and sea level fluctuations, some of which inundated large parts of the LMAV. These climatic pulses generally occurred over millennia, during which time species were able to respond to change.

Influence of Geological History on Ichthyofauna

The large and diverse fish community in the YMD may be attributed to two large-scale features of the Mississippi River basin. The lower Mississippi River basin has remained in its present location as a single large land mass for millions of years over several major geologic time periods and maintained north-south connectivity. Mayden (1988) argues that most species existed before Pleistocene glaciation. Reviewing the fossil records, Miller (1965) suggests that most of the freshwater fish fauna in North America originated shortly before and through the Cenozoic and Pliocene Eras. Sturgeons (Acipenser), bowfin (Amia), and paddlefish (Polydon) were in the drainage since at least the Eocene. Miller (1965) points out that most fossils recovered from the Pleistocene, post-Nebraska glaciation are "indistinguishable from living species." Many of the species listed by Miller (1965) from Pliocene/Pleistocene beds well north of the YMD are common in the present day YMD. Among these are species of buffalo (Ictiobus), two bullheads (Ictalurus melas and I. nebulosus), and several sunfish (Lepomis spp.) and bass (Micropterus spp.). However, Cyprinidae do not appear until during or after the Miocene with many appearing in the Pleistocene (Miller 1965). The north-south orientation of the Mississippi River basin provided both refugia and a center of dispersal for fish during the Pleistocene.

With cooling and glacial advances, fish could move south. For example, species from the Great Lakes were found as far south as Kansas (Smith 1981). During the Wisconsin glaciation, the Mississippi River drainage basin served as a refugium for fishes of the Hudson Bay and central parts of present day Canada (Rempel and Smith 1997). At least 57 species of the Hudson Bay drainage dispersed northward through Lake Agassiz and other glacial lakes eastward along the ice front that developed into the present day Great Lakes (Crossman and McAllister 1986). With rising sea levels that flooded the lower portions of the LMAV and most of the YMD, refuges were available throughout the upper tributaries to the lower Mississippi River (Cross and others 1986).

Geological events and alternating channel morphologies can influence radiation of species within the watershed. The LMAV remained free of glaciers but was exposed to alternating geomorphic patterns and climatic fluctuations between wet and dry regimes (Saucier 1994). Large-scale changes in geomorphic regimes within the drainage as well as frequent re-colonization from refuges could provide sufficient isolation of species for a large-scale species radiation (Smith 1981). Pleistocene glacial advances and retreats alternately connected and isolated large areas. Watersheds were connected by changes in drainage patterns or the formation of large glacial lakes allowing species to disperse. As glaciers retreated and the climate dried, these areas became isolated and species could diverge from their original form. Expansions and contractions of species ranges accompanied these patterns. Mayden (1988) asserts that vicariance was a major process in speciation in the Central Highlands just above the LMAV and at the lead edge of the Pleistocene glaciers. Powers and Warren (2009) suggest a similar mechanism for the endemic Yazoo shiner (*Notropis rafinesquei*).

Braided channels are inherently unstable and shift seasonally depending upon the flood cycle. Channel changes under a meander regime occur over longer time periods, and oxbow lakes and cut-offs that form as a result tend to persist for centuries (Hudson and Kesel 2000, Shankman 1991). For fish to survive in a braided channel regime, they must either locate to more stable environments for part of their life cycle or assume a life cycle with a rapid turnover that can accommodate the dynamics of the physical environment. A large number of species found in the YMD mature at < 120 mm in length and usually do not live longer than 2 or 3 years (Ross 2001). These fish may have been widespread throughout the braided watershed. As the morphology shifted and habitats such as the Sunflower and Yazoo Rivers in the eastern floodplain of the Mississippi became isolated, previous ranges of fish would contract, resulting in localized populations, such as the endemic Yazoo shiner, a species now restricted to the upper Yazoo River basin (Ross 2001).

Habitats formed by meanders in the YMD often are isolated and channels may only flow during high water or at barely measurable velocities between floods. Sloughs and bayous are often hypoxic or anoxic with dissolved oxygen concentrations < 3.0 mg/L, summer temperatures > 35° C, high turbidity, acidic conditions (pH < 5.0), and desiccation (Hoover and Killgore 1998). These conditions require life

history strategies that either use habitats on a temporary basis or have physiological adaptations to withstand these conditions. Most species spawn in the YMD during the spring or early summer during high water (Ross 2001). The blackstripe topminnow (*Fundulus notatus*) uses the thin surface of oxygenated waters during periods of low oxygen and tolerates temperatures up to 42.6 °C (Ross 2001). Several species including chubsuckers (*Erimyzon* spp.), bullheads (*Ameriurus* spp.), and grass pickerel (*Esox americanus*) may be able to switch to anaerobic metabolism, although this is not well documented (Hoover and Killgore 1998). Gars and bowfin have vascularized swim bladders, and bowfin have modified gills to facilitate air breathing (Ross 2001). Other adaptations include tolerance to higher water temperatures, low pH, and turbid water (Hoover and Killgore 1998).

Smith (1981) asserts that we cannot assume "fishes have recently adapted to the environments and climates in which they presently live," and that speciation is generally slower than changes in geography and climate. The fish communities in the LMAV and the YMD have persisted for a long time. The species that remain are those that have physiological adaptations and life cycles that allow them to successfully exploit the processes—hydrologic and geomorphic—and habitats created and maintained during the past several thousands of years. These advantages include tolerances for periods of low dissolved oxygen, high temperatures, and desiccation, as well as movement patterns timed with seasonal flooding.

Phenotypic change occurs over much shorter periods. Thermal tolerance of organisms can change over relatively short (< 40 years) time periods (Skelly and others 2007). Short-lived animals with rapid life cycles often are able to respond more rapidly to changing environmental conditions (Arendt and Wilson 1999). Genetic variation is also important. Small populations with low genetic variation are not likely to respond to rapid environmental changes. However, fishes often display a wide range of phenotypic response to environmental conditions. Pacific salmon (*Oncorhynchus* spp.) occupy a wide range of climatic conditions extending from Alaska to California and show phenotypic variation in response to regional climates (Halupka and others 2003, Hilborn and others 2003). Genetic variation both within and among stocks is a critical factor. Adaptations include return timing for spawning, incubation time, and juvenile residence in freshwater, among others. Phenotypic adaptations of fish in the YMD also are tuned to physical processes. Temperature and floods appear to be among the most influential forces; the former will influence physiological response, whereas, the latter shapes habitats and access to habitats (Finger and Stewart 1987,

Gutreuter and others 1999). Spawning time may be related to floods. Of the 134 species associated with the LMAV, 88 spawn in the spring and of these 27 have extended spawning periods that may continue into the summer or fall (table 1) (Ross 2001). In contrast to many northern species, none in the LMAV spawn in the fall.

Forests of the YMD

The forests of the YMD are the product of a complex geologic and climatic history and of human influences (Delcourt and others 1993). During the past 10,000 years, in response to glacial advances and retreats, pine (*Picea* spp.) forests declined, and oak (*Quercus*) and tupelo (*Nyssa*) forests expanded into the present bottomland hardwood forest ecosystem (Delcourt and Delcourt 1987, Delcourt and others 1993). Seasonal floods have shaped the past and present forest structure and connectivity between the forest and aquatic ecosystems. The chronicles of 16th-century Spanish explorer Hernando DeSoto's exploration include reports of extensive flooding in the YMD (Clayton and others 1993). Geomorphic processes occurring in the YMD created an uneven forest floor contoured with rounded ridges and valleys that vary in heights by 1 to 3 m (Autin and others 1991, Hodges 1994). The uneven forest floor accompanied by seasonal inundation creates a diverse forest structure (Conner and Sharitz 2005). Putnam and others (1960) classified southern hardwood forest into white oak-red oak-hickory associations and sweetgum-water oak associations that generally reflect tolerance to flooding, with the latter group being more tolerant to prolonged flooding. They also identified a third association, riverfront hardwoods, cottonwood (*Populus* sp.), and black willow (*Salix nigra*), that corresponds to riparian habitats.

Riparian habitats are difficult to define in flooded forest environments such as those in the YMD (Howard and Allen 1989). Often riparian forests include all of the bottomland forest (Brinson and others 1981). Howard and Allen (1989) use the term "streamside forest" to avoid the complexity of the definition of "riparian forest" and to provide a context for streamside management for timber harvest; however, distance from the active channel and elevation define the vegetation adjacent to streams and sloughs. The riparian cross section presented by Howard and Allen (1989) begins with baldcypress (*Taxodium distichum*) and tupelo in and along active channel margins followed by overcup oak (*Quercus lyrata*) and water hickory (*Carya aquatica*) in lower depressions in the flood plain. Sweet gum (*Liquidambar styraciflua*) and willow oak (*Q. phellos*) appear on lower natural levees, and swamp chestnut oak (*Q. michauxii*) and cherrybark oak (*Q. falcata*) are on higher

levees. Extensive tracts of cypress were present throughout the sloughs and swamps of the YMD (Saikku 2005).

Canebrakes (giant cane, *Arundinaria gigantea*) were extensive along stream margins when DeSoto arrived in the YMD (Platt and Brantley 1997). The abundance of canebrakes was noted in several other early accounts of the YMD and surrounding area (see table 1 in Platt and Brantley 1997). Canebrakes commonly appear on natural levees where they may be subject to floods but not long periods of submergence (Platt and Brantley 1997). Various sources suggest that canebrakes developed as a result of disturbance by aboriginal agriculture that removed large trees along some sections of streams (Platt and Brantley 1997). Even with aboriginal clearing of streamside forests, extensive tracts of large streamside trees likely remained along stream banks.

Trees in the riparian zone are the primary source of downed wood in the streams and sloughs. Large amounts of wood and downed trees in streams are alluded to in the chronicles of DeSoto's journey as obstacles to navigation (Hudson 1997). Historical accounts of wood in streams in other regions document large jams of wood debris throughout river and stream courses (Bryant and Sedell 1995). Intense logging of the stream banks removed most of the cypress from the stream margins before the late 1880s (Saikku 2005). During this process, most of the large wood in streams was removed as trees were cut and floated to mills downstream. In addition, wood in streams was removed for navigation or in some cases salvaged for wood products (Kaeser and Litts 2008). Riparian trees disappeared as timber harvest expanded into the hardwoods and land was cleared for agriculture, reducing future recruitment of wood in streams. However, large wood jams such as those reported by Shields and others (2000) likely were common throughout the YMD before the 1800s. Killgore[2] reported a persistent log jam in the old channel of the Big Sunflower River near the Red Rock boat ramp. These sparse but large accumulations of large wood are evidence that wood in the streams and bayous of the YMD was extensive before large-scale deforestation occurred.

The extensive hardwood forests near the channels undoubtedly were the source of large amounts of wood in slough and stream channels. Wood enters the streams and bayous from various disturbance events that include wind, ice storms, and bank avulsion. In particular, hurricanes are relatively common events and can place large amounts of wood into the water (Stanturf and others 2007). Living

---

[2] Personal communication 2008 K J Killgore, Research Fishery Biologist, U S Army Corps of Engineers, Waterways Experiment Station, 141 Cane Ridge Road, Vicksburg, MS 39180

Table 1—Fish by family, genus, and species found in the lower Mississippi alluvial flood plain and its subregions

Fam y	Genus	Spec es	Common Name	MS[a]	YMD[b]	BLH[c]	DNF[d]	Stee e[e]
Petromyzont dae	*Ichthyomyzon*	*castaneus*	chestnut amprey	x	x			
Petromyzont dae	*Ichthyomyzon*	*gagei*	southern brook amprey	x				
Petromyzont dae	*Ichthyomyzon*	*unicuspis*	s ver amprey	x				
Petromyzont dae	*Ichthyomyzon*	*aepyptera*	east brook amprey	x				
Ac penser dae	*Scaphirhynchus*	*albus*	pa d sturgeon	x	x			
Ac penser dae	*Scaphirhynchus*	*oxyrinchus*	Gu f sturgeon	r	x			
Ac penser dae	*Scaphirhynchus*	*platorynchus*	shove nose sturgeon	x	x			
Po yodont dae	*Polyodon*	*spathula*	padd ef sh	x	x	x		
Lep soste dae	*Atractosteus*	*spatula*	a gator gar	x	x			
Lep soste dae	*Lepisosteus*	*oculatus*	spotted gar	x	x	x	x	x
Lep soste dae	*Lepisosteus*	*osseus*	ongnose gar	x	x	x	x	x
Lep soste dae	*Lepisosteus*	*platostomus*	shortnose gar	x	x	x	x	x
Am dae	*Amia*	*calva*	bowf n	x	x	x	x	
H odont dae	*Hiodon*	*alosoides*	go deye	x	x			
H odont dae	*Hiodon*	*tergius*	mooneye	r				
Angu dae	*Anguilla*	*rostrata*	Amer can ee	x	x	x		
C upe dae	*Alosa*	*chrysochloris*	sk pjack herr ng	x	x			
C upe dae	*Dorosoma*	*cepedianum*	g zzard shad	x	x			x
C upe dae	*Dorosoma*	*petenense*	threadf n shad	x	x			x
Cypr n dae	*Campostoma*	*anomalum*	centra stonero er	x				
Cypr n dae	*Carassius*	*auratus*	Go df sh (non-nat ve)	x				
Cypr n dae	*Ctenopharyngodon*	*idella*	grass carp (non-nat ve)	x	x			
Cypr n dae	*Cyprinella*	*camura*	b untface sh ner	x			x	
Cypr n dae	*Cyprinella*	*lutrensis*	red sh ner	x	x			x
Cypr n dae	*Cyprinella*	*venusta*	b ackta sh ner	x	x	x	x	x
Cypr n dae	*Cyprinella*	*whipplei*	stee co or sh ner	x				
Cypr n dae	*Cyprinus*	*carpio*	common carp (non-nat ve)	x	x		x	x
Cypr n dae	*Hybognathus*	*hayi*	cypress m nnow	x	x			
Cypr n dae	*Hybognathus*	*nuchalis*	M ss. s very m nnow	x	x			
Cypr n dae	*Notropis*	*amnis*	pa d sh ner	x	x			
Cypr n dae	*Hypopthalmichthys*	*nobiliss*	b ghead carp (non-nat ve)	x	x			
Cypr n dae	*Luxilus*	*chrysocephalus*	str ped sh ner	x	x			
Cypr n dae	*Lythrurus*	*fumeus*	r bbon sh ner	x	x			
Cypr n dae	*Lythrurus*	*roseipinnis*	cherryf n sh ner	x				
Cypr n dae	*Lythrurus*	*umbratilus*	redf n sh ner	x	x			
Cypr n dae	*Macrhybopsis*	*aestivalis*	speck ed chub	x	x			x
Cypr n dae	*Macrhybopsis*	*meeki*	s ck ef n chub	x				
Cypr n dae	*Macrhybopsis*	*storeriana*	s ver chub	x	x			
Cypr n dae	*Notemigonis*	*crysoleucas*	go den sh ner	x	x		x	x
Cypr n dae	*Notropis*	*atherinoides*	emera d sh ner	x	x			x
Cypr n dae	*Notropis*	*blennius*	r ver sh ner	x	x			
Cypr n dae	*Notropis*	*buchanani*	ghost sh ner	x	x			x
Cypr n dae	*Notropis*	*longirostris*	ongnose sh ner	x				
Cypr n dae	*Notropis*	*maculatus*	ta ght sh ner	x	x	x	x	
Cypr n dae	*Notropis*	*sabinae*	sab ne sh ner	x				
Cypr n dae	*Notropis*	*shumardi*	s verband sh ner	x	x			
Cypr n dae	*Notropis*	*texanus*	weed sh ner	x	x			
Cypr n dae	*Notropis*	*volucellus*	m m c sh ner	x	x			
Cypr n dae	*Notropis*	*wickliffi*	channe sh ner	r	x			
Cypr n dae	*Opsopoeodus*	*emiliae*	pugnose m nnow	x	x			x
Cypr n dae	*Phoxinus*	*erythrogaster*	southern redbe y dace	r				
Cypr n dae	*Pimephales*	*notatus*	b untnose m nnow	x	x			
Cypr n dae	*Pimephales*	*promelas*	fathead m nnow	x	x	x		

continued

Table 1—Fish by family, genus, and species found in the lower Mississippi alluvial flood plain and its subregions (continued)

Family	Genus	Species	Common Name	MS[a]	YMD[b]	BLH[c]	DNF[d]	Steele[e]
Cyprinidae	*Pimephales*	*vigilax*	bullhead minnow	x	x		x	
Cyprinidae	*Platygobio*	*gracilis*	flathead chub	x	x			
Cyprinidae	*Semotilus*	*atromaculatus*	creek chub	x	x			
Catostomidae	*Carpiodes*	*carpio*	river carpsucker	x	x			
Catostomidae	*Carpiodes*	*cyprinus*	quillback carpsucker	x	x			
Catostomidae	*Carpiodes*	*velifer*	highfin carpsucker	x	x			
Catostomidae	*Cycleptus*	*elongatus*	blue sucker	x	x			
Catostomidae	*Erimyzon*	*oblongus*	creek chubsucker	x		x		
Catostomidae	*Erimyzon*	*sucetta*	lake chubsucker	x	x	x		
Catostomidae	*Hypentelium*	*nigricans*	northern hogsucker	x	x			
Catostomidae	*Ictiobus*	*bubalus*	smallmouth buffalo	x	x	x	x	x
Catostomidae	*Ictiobus*	*cyprinellus*	bigmouth buffalo	x	x		x	x
Catostomidae	*Ictiobus*	*niger*	black buffalo	x	x	x		x
Catostomidae	*Minytrema*	*melanops*	spotted sucker	x				
Catostomidae	*Moxostoma*	*erythrurum*	golden redhorse	x				
Catostomidae	*Moxostoma*	*poecilurum*	blacktail redhorse	x				
Ictaluridae	*Ameiurus*	*melas*	black bullhead	x	x	x	x	x
Ictaluridae	*Ameiurus*	*natalis*	yellow bullhead	x	x	x	x	x
Ictaluridae	*Ameiurus*	*nebulosus*	brown bullhead	x	x	x		
Ictaluridae	*Ictalurus*	*furcatus*	blue catfish	x	x			
Ictaluridae	*Ictalurus*	*punctatus*	channel catfish	x	x			x
Ictaluridae	*Noturus*	*flavus*	stonecat	x	x			
Ictaluridae	*Noturus*	*gyrinus*	tadpole madtom	x	x	x		x
Ictaluridae	*Noturus*	*hildebrandi*	least madtom	x				
Ictaluridae	*Noturus*	*miurus*	brindled madtom	x				
Ictaluridae	*Noturus*	*nocturus*	freckled madtom	x				
Ictaluridae	*Noturus*	*phaeus*	brown madtom	x				
Ictaluridae	*Noturus*	*stigmosus*	northern madtom	x				
Ictaluridae	*Pylodictis*	*olivaris*	flathead catfish	x	x			
Esocidae	*Esox*	*americanus*	grass pickerel	x	x	x		
Esocidae	*Esox*	*niger*	chain pickerel	x	x	x		
Aphredoderidae	*Aphredoderus*	*sayanus*	pirate perch	x	x	x	x	x
Fundulidae	*Fundulus*	*chrysotus*	golden topminnow	x	x	x	x	x
Fundulidae	*Fundulus*	*dispar*	northern starhead	x	x	x		
Fundulidae	*Fundulus*	*notatus*	blackstripe topminnow	x	x	x		
Fundulidae	*Fundulus*	*olivaceus*	blackspotted topminnow	x	x	x	x	
Poeciliidae	*Gambusia*	*affinis*	western mosquitofish	x	x	x	x	x
Atherinidae	*Labidesthes*	*sicculus*	brook silverside	x	x	x	x	
Atherinidae	*Menidia*	*beryllina*	inland silverside	x	x	x		x
Mugilidae	*Mugil*	*cephalus*	striped mullet	x	x	x		
Moronidae	*Morone*	*chrysops*	white bass	x	x		x	x
Moronidae	*Morone*	*mississippiensis*	yellow bass	x	x			
Elassomatidae	*Elassoma*	*zonatum*	banded pygmy sunfish	x	x	x	x	
Centrarchidae	*Centrarchus*	*macropterus*	flier	x	x	x	x	x
Centrarchidae	*Lepomis*	*cyanellus*	green sunfish	x	x		x	x
Centrarchidae	*Lepomis*	*gulosus*	warmouth	x	x	x	x	x
Centrarchidae	*Lepomis*	*humilis*	orangespotted sunfish	x	x		x	x
Centrarchidae	*Lepomis*	*macrochirus*	bluegill	x	x		x	x
Centrarchidae	*Lepomis*	*marginatus*	dollar sunfish	x	x	x	x	x
Centrarchidae	*Lepomis*	*megalotis*	longear sunfish	x	x			x
Centrarchidae	*Lepomis*	*microlophus*	redear sunfish	x	x		x	

continued

Table 1—Fish by family, genus, and species found in the lower Mississippi alluvial flood plain and its subregions (continued)

Fam y	Genus	Spec es	Common Name	MS[a]	YMD[b]	BLH[c]	DNF[d]	Stee e[e]
Centrarch dae	*Lepomis*	*miniatus*	redspotted sunf sh	x	x	x		
Centrarch dae	*Lepomis*	*symmetricus*	bantam sunf sh	x	x	x	x	x
Centrarch dae	*Micropterus*	*punctulatus*	spotted bass	x	x			
Centrarch dae	*Micropterus*	*salmoides*	argemouth bass	x	x	x	x	x
Centrarch dae	*Pomoxis*	*annularis*	wh te crapp e	x	x		x	x
Centrarch dae	*Pomoxis*	*nigromaculatus*	b ack crapp e	x	x	x	x	x
Perc dae	*Ammocrypta*	*beanii*	naked sand darter	x				
Perc dae	*Ammocrypta*	*clara*	western sand darter	x				
Perc dae	*Ammocrypta*	*vivax*	sca y sand darter	x	x			
Perc dae	*Etheostoma*	*asprigene*	mud darter	x	x			
Perc dae	*Etheostoma*	*caeruleum*	ra nbow darter	x				
Perc dae	*Etheostoma*	*chlorosoma*	b untnose darter	x	x	x		
Perc dae	*Etheostoma*	*fusiforme*	swamp darter	x	x	x	x	
Perc dae	*Etheostoma*	*gracile*	s ough darter	x	x		x	x
Perc dae	*Etheostoma*	*histrio*	har equ n darter	x				
Perc dae	*Etheostoma*	*lynceum*	br ghteye darter	x				
Perc dae	*Etheostoma*	*nigrum*	johnny darter	x	x		x	
Perc dae	*Etheostoma*	*parvipinne*	go dstr pe dar er	x				
Perc dae	*Etheostoma*	*proeliare*	cypress darter	x	x	x		
Perc dae	*Etheostoma*	*stigmaeum*	speck ed darter	x	x			
Perc dae	*Etheostoma*	*swaini*	gu f darter	x				
Perc dae	*Etheostoma*	*artesiae*	ed n darter	x	x			
Perc dae	*Percina*	*caprodes*	ogperch	x	x			
Perc dae	*Percina*	*maculata*	b acks de darter	x				
Perc dae	*Percina*	*sciera*	dusky darter	x				
Perc dae	*Percina*	*shumardi*	r ver darter	x	x			
Perc dae	*Percina*	*vigil*	sadd eback darter	x				
Perc dae	*Stizostedion*	*canadense*	sauger	x	x			
Perc dae	*Stizostedion*	*vitreum*	wa eye	x	x			
Sc aen dae	*Aplodinotus*	*grunniens*	reshwater drum	x	x	x		x

MS = State of Mississippi; YMD = Yazoo Mississippi Delta; BLH = Bottomland Hardwood Forest Aquatic Habitats; DNF = Delta National Forest

[a] Ross (2001)

[b] Killgore and others (2008a)

[c] Hoover and Killgore (1998)

[d] Bryant unpublished data (footno e 4)

[e] Killgore and others (2008b)

trees are an important source of wood in YMD aquatic ecosystems as well. Cypress are long lived and highly resistant to windthrow; however, they are an important element in the structure of aquatic habitat. Their ability to survive long periods with their roots submerged allows them to live in stream channel margins. Their complex root system and fluted buttresses are an important source of "living" large wood in streams Wood from downed trees may be relatively short lived in YMD ecosystems, but living and downed cypress will remain in aquatic systems for centuries (Kaeser and Litts 2008).

Morphology of the YMD

The meander regime and the flood cycle are important processes that influence aquatic habitats in the YMD. They also operate on different time scales. The meander regime, the dominant force shaping flood plain morphology, operates on a scale of centuries and millennia (Fisk 1944, Saucier 1994). Meanders occur as a river migrates across the flood plain creating new channels and abandoning old ones. The abandoned channels form cutoffs that evolve into oxbow lakes. Distributary channels may develop from abandoned channels. Floods, on the other hand, occur on a seasonal cycle and vary in intensity from year to year. Flood effects extend over most of the YMD.

Saucier (1994) identifies six meander LMAV belt stages beginning about 9,500 years BP that traverse the YMD. The chronosequence and locations of the various meander belts are not necessarily precise; however, the evidence is sufficient to show that the meander belts ranged over nearly all of the YMD alluvial flood plain. Over the course of more than 9,000 years, meander belts likely overlapped and older channels were obliterated as new ones were created. Fisk (1944) suggests that some of the earlier belts were derived from the Ohio River, but Saucier (1994) presents more recent evidence that the two rivers did not meander along parallel courses. The aquatic habitats found in the present-day YMD are derived from the meander regimes of the Mississippi River and the smaller rivers within the YMD, such as the Sunflower and Yazoo Rivers (Fisk 1944, Saucier 1994).

Oxbows formed in the meander belts shape the topography of the YMD and are a fundamental part of the development and succession of the aquatic habitat of the YMD (Shankman 1991). Meander scrolls formed by the succession of oxbows across the YMD are a series of curved channels and natural levees formed over thousands of years (Fisk 1944). The curvilinear ridges (meander scrolls) are natural levees of old river banks and are separated by broad depressions from the ancient abandoned river channels (Hupp and others 2005, Shankman 1991). Examples of large oxbow lakes formed by meanders in the Mississippi River are Lake Chicot near Lake Village, AR, and Lake Washington near Greenville, MS. Both lakes are close to the present river course. Smaller oxbow lakes are associated with the adjacent rivers, although many of the lakes have been obliterated by agriculture.

Hooke (2004) proposes five possible mechanisms driving the formation of oxbows. All are related to differential sedimentation and erosion of the river bank with deposition on one bank and erosion on the other, and range from a self-organizing system that has become chaotic to natural evolution of the system and exceptionally high flows that break through narrow points in the meander curves. The mechanisms described by Hooke (2004) do not incorporate the role of large wood in reshaping channels and redirecting river and stream courses (Maser and Sedell 1994). In the smaller rivers of the YMD and possibly in the Mississippi River, large wood accumulations such as those described by Shields and others (2000) would have played an important role in channel morphology of streams and rivers before the effects of intensive human disturbance.

The succession of oxbow lakes occurs over centuries and is not well documented for the YMD. Sedimentation and plant invasions are generally the primary mechanisms for succession. In the bottomland forests of the Southeastern United States, cypress is one of the first tree species to colonize abandoned channels and oxbow lakes. Harper (1912) suggested that cypress could be used to determine the age of succession of aquatic habitats that evolved from oxbow lakes. Shankman (1991) describes the vegetation succession in abandoned channels with cypress colonizing the margins along with willow (*Salix*). Cypress usually persists longer than shorter-lived willow. Seasonal floods will tend to suppress encroachment of vegetation and slow succession. As floods are attenuated, water levels will become lower, allowing greater encroachment of vegetation. Increased sedimentation will increase rates of succession (Richie and others 1983).

Extent and Duration of Historical Flooding

Before construction of the levees, all of the YMD was open to seasonal flooding. The area flooded was regulated by the height of the floodwaters and the topography of the land. The entire area quite likely was not flooded each year. In the unconstrained flood plain, floodwaters flowed laterally across the flood plain, following the contours of the land (Junk and others 1989). The same process would have occurred in the YMD as the Mississippi River, the Yazoo River, and the major distributary streams flooded. As the floodwaters flowed across the flood plain, isolated oxbows, sloughs, and swamps were connected.

Seasonal floods in the YMD are driven by hydrologic events, i.e., precipitation and snowmelt, in the upper watershed of the Mississippi River and by regional events. Annual cycles of precipitation and snowmelt are related to climatic patterns (Franklin and others 2003). The geographic separation also tends to extend the duration of the flood season, which can extend from January through May (fig. 3) (http://countrystudies.us/united-states/weather. Date accessed: August 2008). Early in the season, high flows are from rainfall in the YMD and surrounding highlands (fig. 4). Later in the season, April through June, the flood pulse in the YMD is driven by precipitation, including spring snowmelt in the upper Mississippi River basin. The peak discharge in the Mississippi River increases through spring as snowmelt in the upper watershed of the Mississippi accompanies high precipitation in spring (fig. 3 and fig. 4).

Although events upstream affect hydrology downstream, interannual variation differed between the upper and lower Mississippi River (Franklin and others 2003). The within-

Mississippi River
Mean Discharge (m³/sec)
1932-1998

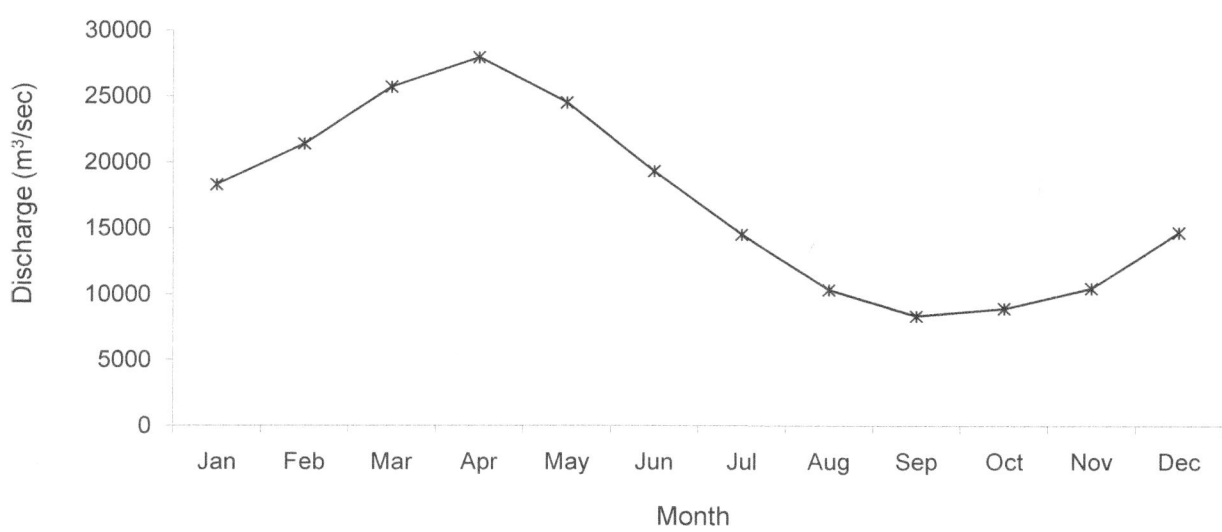

Figure 3—Mean monthly discharge for the Mississippi River over a period of 66 years.

Average Rainfall in YMD

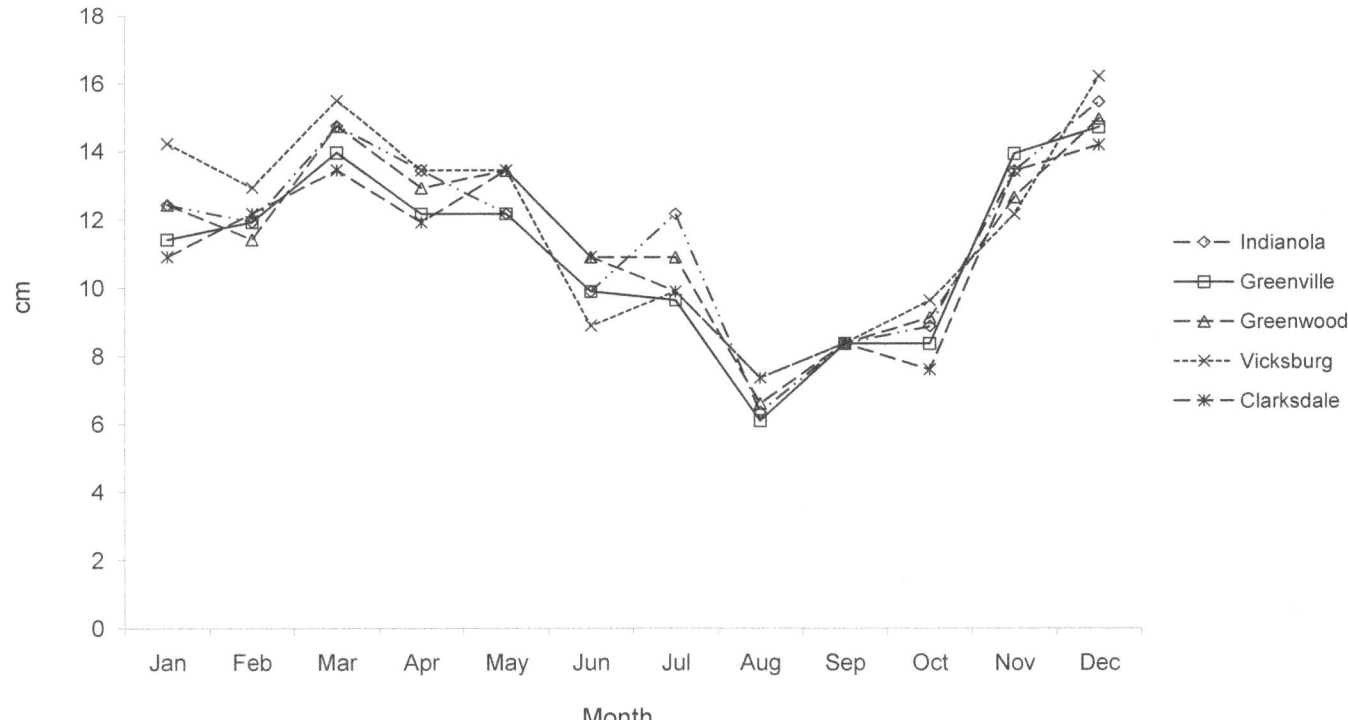

Figure 4—Mean monthly rainfall for five locations throughout the YMD. http://countrystudies.us/united-states/weather. [Date accessed: August 2008].

year pattern of higher flows in the river is from February to June followed by six months of lower flows (Franklin and others 2003). This pattern is consistent between the upper and lower sections of the river. Levees, dams, and meander cutoff have substantially altered the natural pattern of flooding on the YMD.

Effects of Seasonal Flooding on Habitats

The flood pulse connects the flood plain to the river (Barko and others 2006, Galat and others 1998, Goulding 1980, Junk and others 1989). Junk and others (1989) characterized the lateral movement of water across the flood plain as a moving littoral zone. As the flood pulse moved across the flood plain of the YMD, perennial aquatic habitats that include oxbows, swamps, bayous, and distributary channels (e.g., Deer Creek and the Sunflower River) were connected to the Mississippi River. Floodwaters flowed into ephemeral channels and depressions in bottomland forests and connected these to perennial habitats. The life cycle of many aquatic organisms is linked closely to the timing of the flood pulse.

The flood pulse functions both as a transport mechanism and a transport corridor. As floodwater moves across the flood plain, it alters the water chemistry of previously isolated aquatic habitats, carries inorganic and organic material across the flood plain, and replenishes water in pools and isolated sloughs (Amoros and Bornette 2002, Ewing 1991, Junk and others 1989, Schramm and Eggleton 2006, Tockner and others 1999). In the Atchafalaya River basin in southeastern Louisiana, water temperatures decreased and dissolved oxygen increased, as did organic carbon, with a resulting increase in the abundance of planktonic rotifers as floodwaters covered the flood plain (Holland and others 1983). They concluded that the flushing of backwater habitats by the flood pulse was an important factor in maintaining planktonic diversity. Larval fish may be subject to passive movement during flooding; however, larger mobile species may use the flood pulse as a transportation corridor (Killgore and Baker 1996, Sheaffer and Nickum 1986, Turner and others 1994). Ross and Baker (1983) identified the group of species that moved into the flood plain for feeding or spawning as "flood exploitive." In the Atchafalaya River in Louisiana, spotted gar (*Lepisosteus oculatus*) migrated into flood plain habitats with the spring floods to spawn (Snedden and others 1999). More than 62 species were captured in natural (i.e., unleveed) flood plain habitats associated with the Mississippi River near Louisiana (Guillory 1979). Before the levees along the Mississippi River, the flood pulse provided a corridor from the main

channel to the aquatic habitats in the flood plain of the YMD (Puth and Wilson 2001).

During dry periods, the flood plain and the main channel existed as separate entities within the watershed. Increased connectivity also may increase similarity among habitats (Thomaz and others 2007). Thomaz and others (2007) suggested that the variation in many physical/chemical measures decreased with increasing connectivity during floods. Similarity among fish communities would increase with greater access as well. Differences among habitats increase with time as flood frequency and intensity decrease and habitats remain isolated for longer periods of time. If habitats are isolated for longer periods of time—many years versus annual—differences in physical attributes and biological communities would increase. Temperatures will increase and dissolved oxygen concentrations will decrease as habitats are isolated for longer periods of time. Both of these trends tend to be detrimental to most fishes, as well as many amphibians and other aquatic organisms (Matthews 1987, Smale and Rabeni 1995). Deterioration of water quality and loss of connectivity will decrease biological diversity in isolated habitats (Capone and Kushlan 1991, Rutherford and others 2001).

Seasonal floods redistribute fishes throughout flooded habitats. Even under present conditions, oxbow lakes that are connected to the Mississippi River support a different species assemblage than those that are isolated (Miranda 2005). Before the levees, unconstrained flooding linked habitats throughout the YMD to the Mississippi River. The winter and spring floods provided pathways for fish dispersal throughout the YMD. In a recent flood event in the upper Mississippi River, Barko and others (2006) observed 42 species of fishes that dispersed into a flood plain. As habitats become connected, diversity among habitats decreased, but biodiversity throughout the flood plain may become greater than habitats that are not flooded periodically (Thomaz and others 2007).

Distribution of Fish in the YMD Before the Levees

No records exist of the fish communities in the YMD before the levees existed. However, observations based on the archaeological record show that fish were an important part of the diet of aboriginal people. This record also shows that certain species were widespread over the YMD. The fish most likely were collected as food and represent larger taxa. As a result, the list is far from a random sample of the species assemblage. The archeological record is also biased by collection methods, sampling intensity, and identification procedures. Furthermore, fish were captured by a range of methods by aboriginal people (Scott 1995). The best record is from the Rock Levee Site approximately 400 to 900 C.E. (current era) located along the Mississippi River near Clarksdale, MS (Scott 1995). The site was sampled intensively, and among more than 39,000 bone fragments, 25,502 were from 31 fish taxa. Most were identified to species; the rest were identified to genera (table 2). Of these, catfishes (*Ictaluridae*) and suckers (*Catostomidae*) comprised 28 percent and 21 percent, respectively. They were followed by sunfish (*Lepomis* spp.), bowfin, and gars at 18 percent, 15 percent, and 10 percent, respectively (Scott 1995). Bowfin and gars were present at the other sites where fish samples were identified; catfishes were present at two other sites, one of which was located near the Yazoo River. Gars, bowfin, basses (Centrarchids), and sunfishes (Centrarchids) were present at the Palusha Creek site near Greenwood, MS, along the Yazoo River.

The species assemblages from these sites often represent samples from time spans that extend over hundreds of years from a single site. During this time, surrounding habitats may have changed. For example, a bayou or river cutoff may have evolved into an oxbow lake or a slough from one sample strata to the next. Present analysis of the samples has not proceeded to a point where a time sequence can be reliably identified.[3]

With few exceptions, fish found at the various archeological sites throughout the YMD are still present, and most are, or appear to be, reasonably abundant. Sauger (*Stizostedion canadense*) and possibly walleye (*Stizostedion* spp.) (table 2) are either absent or extremely rare in the YMD, although they are reported in the lower Mississippi River drainage (Ross 2001). Their presence in archeological remains suggests that they were more common during aboriginal times (about 500 C.E.). One explanation for their decline may be that the climate was cooler during this period; however, water quality and habitat conditions were undoubtedly more conducive to these species as well. Spotted bullhead (*Ameriurus serracanthis*) was reported from one site in Leflore County, Mississippi. It is not listed in Ross (2001) but does occur in southeastern Alabama (Boschung and Mayden 2004).

The archeological record provides sufficient evidence that fishes were an important part of the diet of aboriginal people in the YMD. For that to be the case, fishes had to have been abundant. Given the massive loss of aquatic habitats from anthropogenic activity in the past 300 years, it can be easily concluded that the number of fish was substantially greater than the number at present. Further, aquatic habitats were qualitatively different than present, which would affect fish communities. Channels with well-developed riparian forests, including hardwoods along the bank and cypress in and along the stream margin, would lead to highly complex habitats with abundant large wood. With the absence of large tracts of industrial agricultural lands, sediment recruitment into bayous and stream was lower and, without flood control dams, was flushed out more readily. The ubiquity of gars and bowfin in the archeological remains suggests that low dissolved oxygen and high temperatures were present in at least some habitats. Greater connectivity between the flood plain and the rivers would improve water quality and provide access to the flood plain for spawning and rearing. This, in turn, would contribute to greater numbers of species.

Post-European Habitats of the YMD

The landscape of the YMD has a long history of anthropogenic disturbance. Humans were present in the YMD perhaps as early as 14,000 to 10,000 years ago and developed agriculture in the flood plain about 2,000 years ago (Delcourt 1987, Saikku 2005). For the most part, forest clearing for agriculture was concentrated along river and slough corridors in the flood plains and adjacent terraces (Delcourt 1987, Delcourt and others 1993), but it probably had only localized influence on the flood plain dynamics and did little to disrupt the natural rhythms of seasonal flood pulses of the river. However, Peacock and others (2004) suggest that sediment from aboriginal agriculture may have been responsible for a decline in freshwater mussel populations. With the collapse of aboriginal populations in the 1500s, aboriginal clearings were recolonized by hardwood forests (Hamel and Buckner 1998). The onset of European settlement brought large-scale land clearing and intensive agricultural development during the 1800s. By the 1840s, intensive timber harvest was underway (Saikku 2005). High-value baldcypress along waterways such as Steele Bayou and the bayous between Deer Creek and the Sunflower River were harvested first (Saikku 2005). Conversion of forest land to agriculture was a major part of deforestation of the YMD as well. Currently, bottomland hardwood forests comprise < 17 percent of the remaining land in the YMD.

Three interrelated primary anthropogenic forces that altered the landscape and aquatic habitats in the YMD—flood

---

[3] Personal communication 2007 E Jackson, Professor, Dept of Anthropology and Sociology, University of Southern Mississippi, 118 College Drive, Hattiesburg, MS 39406

Table 2—Species recovered in archaeological sites in the Yazoo Mississippi Delta (YMD)

Taxa	Common name	RL	WC	MC	FR	PC	LW
Amia calva	Bowfin	x	x	x	x	x	x
Lepisosteus sp.	Gar	x	x	x	x	x	x
L. osseus	Longnose gar	x			x		
Atractosteus spatula	Alligator gar	x			x		
Clupeidae	Shad/herring	x				x	
Alosa sp.	Shad/herring	x					
Dorosoma cepedianum	Gizzard shad	x					
Esox sp.	Pickerel	x				x	
Cyprinidae	Minnow	x		x		x	
Catostomidae	Sucker	x		x		x	x
Moxostoma sp.	Redhorse			x			
Ictiobus bubalus	Smallmouth buffalo	x					
I. cyprinellus	Bigmouth buffalo	x	x				
Minytrema melanops	Spotted sucker	x					
Ictalurus spp.	Catfish	x		x	x		x
Ictalurus punctatus	Channel catfish	x	x	x			x
I. furcatus	Blue catfish	x					
I. melas	Black bullhead	x					
I. natalis	Yellow bullhead	x					
Ameriurus spp.	Bullheads			x		x	
Ameriurus nebulosus	Brown bullhead				x	x	
A. natalis	Yellow bullhead				x		
A. serracanthis	Spotted bullhead				x		
Pylodictis olivaris	Flathead catfish	x		x			
Perciformes	Perch	x					
Probably Morone						x	
Morone sp.	White/Yellow bass	x					
Morone chrysops					x		
Centrarchidae	Sunfish	x		x			x
Micropterus sp.	Bass	x				x	
Micropterus salmoides	Largemouth bass	x	x				
M. punctulatus	Spotted bass	x					
Lepomis sp.	Sunfish	x	x			x	
Lepomis microlophus	Redear sunfish	x					
L. macrochirus	Bluegill		x		x	x	
L. gulosus	Warmouth				x		
Pomoxis sp.	Crappie	x				x	
Stizostedion	Sauger/walleye	x					
Stizostedion canadense	Sauger	x					
Aplodinotus sp.	Freshwater drum	x	x	x	x		X
Chaenobryttus spp. = *Lepomis gulosus*	Warmouth				x		

RL = Rock evee s te (400-1400 C E) (Scott 1995); WC = We come Center (1-1500 C E) (Mooney and others 2003); MC = Mckn ght (900-1200 C E) (Bre tburg 1998); FR = French s te (100-1200 C E) (W son 1987; PC = Pa usha Creek (500-900 C E) (Brown and others 1994); LW = Law s te (1100-1500 C E) (Coxe 1999) control levees, deforestation, and large-scale agriculture—occurred during the past 150 years. The levees isolated the larger rivers from their flood plains and effectively stopped the creation of new oxbow lakes. Deforestation removed riparian trees as well as trees in the water such as cypress. Recent large-scale industrial agriculture changed landscape topography from small ridges and valleys formed by meander scrolls to large areas of level fields. Bayous, streams, and tributaries were dredged and straightened to remove water from the land. Small oxbows and sloughs were filled or isolated. Over a period of < 150 years, the flood plain was effectively decoupled from the Mississippi and Yazoo Rivers.

Hydrology

The hydrology of the YMD has changed substantially from pre-European conditions. Massive flood control projects, in conjunction with engineering projects to ensure navigation routes, have included dredging in the main channel, wood removal (snagging), removal of channel meanders, bank stabilization, and construction of a massive levee system that extends along most of the Mississippi and Yazoo Rivers (Brown and others 2005, Jackson and Ye 2000). Water control structures have been installed throughout the streams and bayous of the YMD as flood control and water management efforts, further isolating habitats. In addition, large-scale pump projects move water from rivers such as the Little Sunflower River onto wetlands to coincide with waterfowl use. Diversion channels have been built throughout the YMD to carry excess water during floods and often carry water throughout the year. These measures are effective for flood control (Kemper 1928) but have decoupled the flood pulse from the flood plain.

Levees, dams, and meander cutoffs along and in the Mississippi and Yazoo Rivers have altered the timing and intensity of hydrological processes of the YMD (Brown and others 2005). The purpose of the structures is to keep water off developed lands in the flood plain (agricultural, urban, and suburban areas). The levees along the Mississippi River have effectively stopped lateral movement of the flood pulse across the historic flood plain. In all recent flood events since 1927, the lateral movement of the Mississippi River has been restricted to the area between the river bank and the levees, also known as "batture land." By concentrating floodwaters in a smaller area, water rises faster and velocities are higher on the land between the river and the levees. Lateral flooding of the flood plain is restricted primarily to the sections of distributary channels without levees (e.g., Sunflower River, Steele Bayou). Dams on the major tributaries of the Yazoo

River attenuate spring flows across the YMD. The example from the Sardis lake dam shows the higher flows in the Little Tallahatchie River above the dam from December through April and decreasing into the summer; below the dam, low flows occur in April and increase through the summer (fig. 5). Cutoffs and reservoirs reduce the intensity and change the duration of winter and spring floods. In the Mississippi River, meander cutoffs increase channel incision and reduce peak flows (Biedenharn and others 2000). Natural bayous and tributaries have been modified to remove water from agricultural land as rapidly as possible, usually by changing them from meanders to linear drainage ditches. Diversion and storage of water extend the amount of time water remains on flooded areas. Smaller areas are flooded for longer periods of time.

As a result, a large part of the historical flood plain is no longer exposed to the flood pulse of the Mississippi. The result is that the rise and fall of floodwaters on the flood plain are disconnected from the rise and fall of floodwaters in the river. Franklin and others (2003) concluded that intra-annual periodicity of flooding in the Mississippi River was not altered by flood control alterations, but high and low flow events tended to be less variable and were lower and higher, respectively, than events before 1929 that were used as the before control period. The timing and duration of the flood pulse may approximate historical conditions, but the effect across the flood plain is greatly different. Many areas receive less flooding for shorter periods, whereas other areas may receive more for longer periods.

Aquatic Habitats of the YMD

Virtually all aquatic habitats in the YMD have been subjected to intensive anthropogenic modification, either physical or hydrologic, and usually both. More than 80 percent of the land in the YMD is used for large-scale agriculture (Killgore and others 2008b). Most of the remaining land is urban or suburban and is protected from large-scale floods. An undocumented number of sloughs, swamps, and small natural ponds have been obliterated. Larger oxbow lakes remain but are subjected to high rates of sedimentation from surrounding agricultural land. Streams and sloughs that flow through agricultural land have been altered and now have either no riparian trees or only a small band of 10 m or less. As a result, few areas in the YMD provide habitat conditions that are similar to those present before European settlement.

The largest contiguous tract of bottomland hardwood forest (24,700 ha) in the YMD is in the Delta National

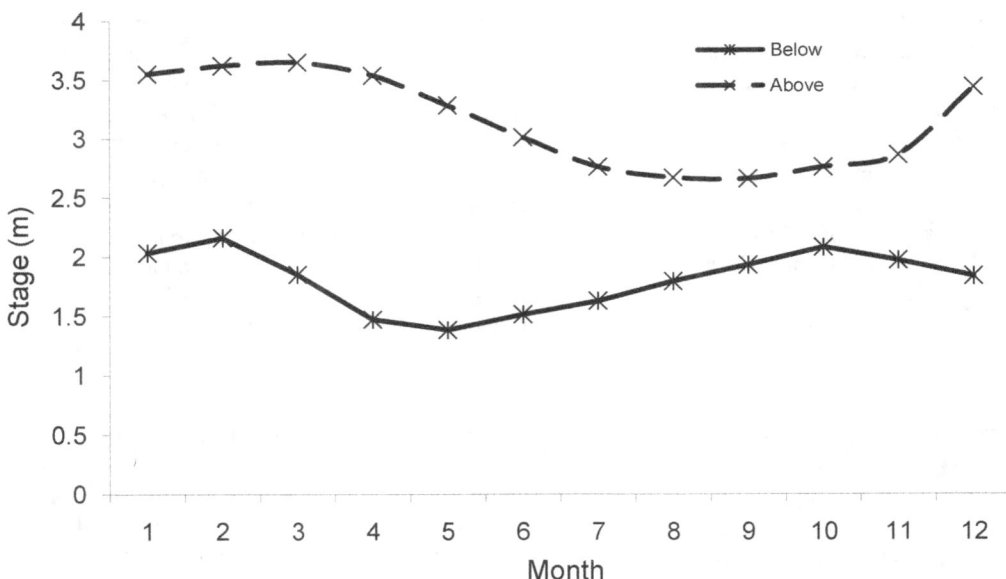

Above and Below Sardis Dam

Figure 5—Mean monthly stages for 2008 above and below the Sardis Dam from the Batesville (below) and Etta (above) gages.

Forest (DNF). Patches of forests also occur in the 40,400 ha in the Theodore Roosevelt National Wildlife Refuge Complex, which comprises seven units and includes active and abandoned agricultural land. Patches of forest also exist on private lands; however, these are usually intensively managed for timber production and often are reclaimed agricultural land. The result is a highly fragmented mosaic of forest land in the YMD. For fish, the primary corridors are the rivers and bayous that eventually flow into the Mississippi River. Large tracts of privately owned timberland are present in the batture land between the Mississippi River and the levees, and these areas are regularly exposed to seasonal flooding.

With the widespread construction of levees, a new ecosystem was created in the land between the river and the levees (Stanturf and Schoenholtz 1998). The aquatic landscape of the YMD may be separated into the batture lands and the historic flood plain outside the levees. Both are distinct with respect to their exposure to flooding. Oxbow lakes are the dominant natural aquatic habitat in the batture lands (Miranda 2005). Most other aquatic habitats such as ponds formed from borrow pits are the result of anthropogenic activities generally associated with the construction and maintenance of the levees or with river control measures such as dredging or wing-dike construction. Some of these listed by Baker and

others (1991) are flood plain ponds that may be perennial or ephemeral, seasonally flooded tributaries, and borrow pits. Borrow pits and side channels may retain water after floodwaters recede and can provide refuge habitat for fish (Hoover and Killgore 2002).

The aquatic habitats in the flood plain are either rivers that developed during deglaciation of the upper watershed or habitats that were derived from the meander belt of the river (Autin and others 1991). Lotic habitats are separated into three groups: rivers, bayous, and tributaries. Lentic habitat types include oxbow lakes, ponds, sloughs, and swamps. In the YMD, most of the lentic habitats were derived from meanders. Oxbow lakes form when a meander cutoff, the meander bend, is blocked at the upstream end of the cutoff. Over time the oxbow lake is isolated from the river channel and fills with sediment, and ultimately vegetation encroaches across the lake as it fills with sediment. In a forest setting, succession in oxbow lakes occurs over thousands of years. With disturbance events that increase sediment rates, the process proceeds more rapidly (Richie and others 1983). This has important consequences for habitats located in the flood plain isolated by levees (Miranda and Lucas 2004). Levees effectively halt the meander process in the flood plain that they isolate and prevent future development of oxbow lakes.

No definitive system of habitat classification for the YMD or alluvial flood plain habitats appears to exist. Names and criteria for classification often differ among studies; six are listed by Baker and others (1991). Baker and others (1991) define sloughs as remnants of abandoned river channels that have water in them throughout the year. They may either be connected or disconnected from the river and are differentiated from oxbow lakes primarily on the basis of size. Hodges (1994) defined sloughs as shallow depressions that collect water but eventually dry out. They are characterized by baldcypress and swamp tupelo. Turner and others (1994) separated habitats into "low-no flow" (bayous and sloughs) and "main river," e.g., the Mississippi River.

Habitats listed in table 3 are adapted from distinctions by Baker and others (1991) that separate naturally occurring habitats into flowing (lotic) and pond (lentic) habitats that have perennial water (Baker and others 1991, Killgore and Hoover 1992). Lotic habitats, such as the Sunflower River and the Steele, Howell, and Black bayous, drain the YMD and flow into the Yazoo or Mississippi Rivers. Although rivers and bayous have been altered by various land use practices, their distribution is relatively unaffected by land use. Oxbow lakes are the dominant lentic habitat in the YMD. Their distribution is dictated by distance from the Mississippi River; however, oxbows are also formed by interior rivers such as the Sunflower and Yazoo Rivers. Their numbers decrease with distance from the river, as does their connectivity with the river (Miranda 2005). Smaller habitats such as sloughs, pools, and swamps are uncommon on developed land, but are common throughout forested land found on public lands such as the DNF and the various national wildlife refuges in the YMD.

Land use patterns affect habitat quality as well as distribution of aquatic habitat. Sediment and chemicals associated with agriculture are among the most significant stressors in aquatic habitats in the YMD. These two stressors have resulted in lower species diversity in lotic habitats of the YMD (Killgore and others 2008b). Higher sediment deposition also occurs in oxbow lakes surrounded by agricultural land (Richie and others 1983). Increased nutrient loading from agricultural runoff contributes to eutrophication of aquatic habitats resulting in anoxic conditions. Algal blooms driven by the input of nutrients from agricultural activity produce huge variation in dissolved oxygen concentrations, with conditions capable of ranging from supersaturation during the day to anoxic conditions at night (Shields and others, no date).

Riparian corridors through developed land are commonly devoid of trees in the YMD. Associated with the absence of streamside trees is the paucity of instream large wood, an important element in the biotic community of streams in the Southern United States (Benke and others 1985, Wallace and Benke 1984, Warren and others 2002). In contrast, bayous flowing through forested lands appear to have greater amounts of instream large wood from standing live

Table 3—Perennial aquatic habitats of the YMD

Name	Type	Description	Source
Slough	Lentic/Lotic	Narrow, shallow < 3 m; may be connected to main channel (contiguous); mud substrate	Baker and others 1991
Oxbow lake	Lentic	Large (200 to > 3500 ha) up to 1 m wide and 25 km long; may stratify during the summer	Baker and others 1991
Flood plain pond/swamp	Lentic	May be low points in intermittent tributaries (< 500 m^2); mud substrate with abundant organic debris	Baker and others 1991
Tributary	Lotic	Small (< 6 m wide approximate); flow into larger streams (e.g., Sunflower, Deer Creek) within the YMD; may drain forested wetlands or modified into agricultural drainage ditches	
Distributary channel/river	Lotic	Larger channels (> 6 m wide) within the boundaries of the YMD that drain the flood plain	
Main channel rivers	Lotic	Mississippi River; Yazoo River	

Figure 6—Ten-mile Bayou, Delta National Forest, with large wood and riparian trees on bank and in the channel.

baldcypress and downed streamside trees (fig. 6). Riparian shading tends to suppress aquatic macrophyte growth. Small tributaries and ponds, as well as swamps, are distributed throughout forested habitats that have not been previously exposed to agriculture. These areas tend to be inundated during spring floods and may be important seasonal spawning and nursery areas for flood-dependent species (Killgore and Baker 1996, Sheaffer and Nickum 1986).

Fish Populations in the YMD

The LMAV supports a highly diverse fish community within the highly diverse fish community of the Southeastern United States (Warren and others 2000). Ross (2001) lists 134 species for the LMAV within the State of Mississippi. Of these, 102 are reported for the YMD (table 1). The list for the YMD includes paddlefish and sturgeons that are found primarily in the Sunflower, Yazoo, and Mississippi Rivers. Hoover and Killgore (1998) list 40 species associated with bottomland hardwood forests, but the list is derived from relatively few studies, most of which are outside the YMD.

More than 70 species were reported for the bottomland hardwood forests near the Cache River, Arkansas (Killgore and Hoover 1992). This is one of the few remaining large tracts of bottomland hardwood forest in the LMAV. In a recent survey of habitats in the DNF, 37 species were captured with seines and backpack electrofishing equipment.[4]

The wide range of life history characteristics is manifested in the species diversity found in the LMAV and the YMD. Ross (2001) provides a synopsis of the life history characteristics of all fish known from the State of Mississippi based on a wide range of literature. However, few studies are from the YMD. Some useful characteristics for various assessment projects are habitat use, trophic guild, and reproductive strategy. Habitat was used by Ross and Baker (1983), who separate species into "flood exploitive"

[4]Bryant, M D ; Warren, M L 2008 Floods, forests, and fishes in the Delta National Forest, Mississippi: a study of fish assemblages in the Delta National Forest and nearby aquatic habitats 25 p Unpublished manuscript On file with: Center for Bottomland research, P O Box 227, Stoneville, MS 38776

and "flood quiescent" on the basis of the movement of species in response to flooding, a classification that Kwak (1988) uses to identify fish that moved into flood plain habitats during high water. Many of these fish were juveniles. Other studies in bottomland hardwood forests near the YMD show that the flooded forest habitats are used for spawning and rearing during the first year of life for a range of species (Killgore and Baker 1996). Killgore and Hoover (1992) identify four reproductive strategies (pelagic, benthic, vegetation, and crevice spawning) and three habitat types (oxbow lakes, flood plain ponds, and flowing water) to develop a matrix that describes fish species assemblages. Hoover and Killgore (1998) review a range of studies on fish of forested wetlands, identifying life history characteristics that include morphology, physiology, reproduction, and predation. Of these studies, only two were located in Mississippi and one in the most northern part of the YMD. Studies of sport fish in larger oxbow lakes are more numerous.

Oxbow lakes are important to recreational fishing in the YMD (Miranda 2005, Miranda and Lucas 2004). Miranda and Lucas (2004) identified 61 species (> 70 mm) in 29 lakes in the LMAV. Sunfish and bluegills (*L. macrochirus*) in particular dominated the catch (> 50 percent). Largemouth bass (*Micropterus salmoides*) (9 percent) and black (*Pomoxis nigromaculatus*) and white crappie (*Pomoxis annularis*) (7 percent) were also important species. All are considered sport fish. Fish communities appear to be influenced by turbidity and lake morphology. Temperate bass (*Morone* spp.), black crappie, redear sunfish (*Lepomis microlophus*), warmouth (*L. gulosus*), and gar (*Lepisosteus* spp.) tended to be associated with less turbid waters (Miranda and Lucas 2004).

In a similar study, Miranda (2005) observed a relationship between connectivity to the Mississippi River and fish communities. Fish often associated with flowing water were more common in lakes with greater connectivity. These included skipjack herring (*Alosa chrysochloris*), river carpsucker (*Carpoides carpio*), and white bass (*Morone chrysops*). During this study, all species captured in lakes outside the levees also were captured in lakes within the levees (Miranda 2005). Seven species were captured only in lakes between the levees and the river: skipjack herring, river carpsucker, highfin carpsucker (*Carpoides velifer*), spotted sucker (*Minytrema melonops*), striped bass (*Morone saxatilis*), flier (*Centrarchus macropterus*), and grass carp (*Ctenopharyngodon idella*). Of these, only the flier was captured in the survey of the DNF. Smaller fish (< 70 mm) with shorter life cycles were not sampled in the studies of

oxbow lakes. Oxbow lakes within the batture lands support different fish communities than those in the flood plain (Stanturf and Schoenholtz 1998). This appears to be related to turbidity, but frequent connection to the river would also influence the fish community.

Fish in the YMD are a significant part of the cultural heritage of the region. Fish are caught in artesian fisheries (small-scale commercial fisheries) and recreational fisheries (Jackson 2004). Artesian fisheries tend to be low-profit enterprises but are an important part of the lifestyle of residents of the region. They target larger individuals of the three buffalo species (*Ictiobius* spp.) and three species of catfish: blue catfish (*Ictalurus furcatus*), channel catfish (*I. punctatus*) and flathead catfish (*Pylodictus olivaris*). The legal limits reported by Jackson (2004) are 410 mm and 305 mm for buffalos and catfish, respectively. Gar, bowfin, several centrarchids, and catfish are part of the recreational fishery (Jackson 2005). Within the centrarchid group are a variety of sunfish (*Lepomis* spp.), black basses (*Micropterus* spp.), and both species of crappies (*Pomoxis* spp.). Although most are caught with hook and line, larger catfish are caught by hand grappling, a technique unique to the Southeastern United States (Jackson and others 1997). As a group, these fisheries represent an important part of the social and economic life of the region.

The landscape of the YMD is modified extensively by human activity and, as a result, diversity is likely to be lower in the YMD than in many forested habitats elsewhere in the LMAV. Few published studies exist for fish or aquatic habitat in the YMD. In a recent evaluation of a restoration project on Steele Bayou, north of Vicksburg, MS, Killgore and others (2008b) reported an increase in the number of fish species captured from 20 to 30 species following the removal of soft substrate, sediment abatement, and bank stabilization (Killgore and others 2008b). Notably, the number of species intolerant of poor water quality increased after the project. Overlap occurred between the fish communities at Steele Bayou and the DNF, with 25 species in common (table 1). Of the 34 species captured in the DNF, only 4 are classified as intolerant of low water quality, but 26 are classified as moderately tolerant or tolerant of lower water quality.

Management of Aquatic Habitat in the YMD

Until recently, little attention was given to management of habitats for aquatic resources in the YMD. Protection of riparian areas and aquatic habitats is relatively piecemeal and is often directed at creating wildlife or waterfowl habitat. Creation of buffer strips or management zones along streams and sloughs flowing through private lands is voluntary. Conservation reserve and wetland reserve programs (CRP, WRP) are based on economic incentives, whereby the landowner is paid for lost revenue from land that is set aside from agriculture to create a buffer area. Smaller tracts of public lands represented by National Forests (U.S. Department of Agriculture Forest Service), Wildlife Management Areas (U.S. Department of the Interior, Fish and Wildlife Service), and State parks exist as patches throughout the YMD. These occupy a relatively small part of the land base (< 3.7 percent) and have varying management objectives. Most riparian areas and aquatic habitats are exposed to a wide range of effects that accompany extensive and intensive agricultural development.

Given the present condition of aquatic habitat in the YMD, restoration is a high management priority. Killgore and others (2008b) identified three stressors that arise from agricultural practices in the YMD: deforestation, increased sediment, and reduced stream flow. In Steele Bayou, Killgore and others (2008b) proposed restoration procedures to increase summer water storage, to remove soft substrate, and to create riparian buffers that address three principal stressors operating: water level management, soft substrate, and lack of suitable riparian habitat. Steele Bayou is representative of many bayous and streams in the YMD, and these measures have utility for restoring habitats elsewhere. Broader issues remain with respect to improving aquatic conditions throughout the YMD.

Agriculture and flood control impose multiple stressors on the aquatic habitat of the YMD. The National Research Council (NRC 1992) identified a set of stressors for lakes and flowing waters that incorporates those of Killgore and others (2008b) and includes hydrologic and morphological modifications, erosion and siltation, water quality, and introduction of exotic species. Flow mistiming is a hydrological stressor that affects connectivity between mainstream rivers and flood plain habitats and retention of water on the flood plain. Morphological modifications include loss of riparian vegetation and trees, dredging, and channelization. Excessive erosion and sedimentation affect substrate quality and are related to agricultural erosion and bank destabilization. Deterioration of water quality arises from increased nutrient levels and toxic compounds that are incorporated into the biota. A suite of additional symptoms of deteriorating water quality includes decreased concentrations of dissolved oxygen, low pH, and increased water temperatures. Exotic species often have an adverse effect on native species and frequently are better adapted

to deteriorating habitat and water quality (Jackson and Mandrak 2002, Meador and others 2005, Schade and Bonar 2005).

These stressors are interrelated, and some can be addressed by managing land use practices. Modification of land management practices is an important prerequisite to restoration of natural processes to aquatic habitats in the YMD. The NRC (1992) provides a generalized approach to restoration and specific examples. A key element in their approach is to conduct a triage to identify priorities. They also give a detailed list of requisites for project design and implementation, including identification of goals and objectives, an economic evaluation, collection of baseline information, a monitoring plan, and selection of criteria to measure performance. They also offer a feedback mechanism for use during project implementation that facilitates ongoing evaluation and modifications where needed. The post-project evaluation is designed to determine how well objectives were achieved, what was learned from the project, and how the design could be improved or modified for future projects. The realities of the landscape and socioeconomics of the YMD are such that little probability exists of restoring large areas of the YMD to pre-European conditions.

The definition of *restoration* by the NRC is to transform an ecosystem to close to its state before anthropogenic modification, a difficult if not impossible task for the aquatic ecosystems of the YMD (National Research Council 1992). Sparks and others (1998) applied the term *naturalization* to their approach to improve conditions in the upper Mississippi River. The goal was to move aquatic ecosystem processes closer to natural conditions within the context of socioeconomic constraints. They used manipulation of flows in their example. Reestablishing riparian vegetation and trees along streams and bayous in the YMD is an example of a "naturalization" project that could be applied in the YMD. Riparian trees can recreate natural processes of shading, large wood recruitment, and instream structure to bayous and sloughs with degraded channels. Some naturalization projects and their outcomes appear to be intuitive and relatively straightforward to implement. However, in the case of sediment reduction, evaluation and measurement are more complex, and results may not be straightforward (Shields 2008). As defined, "naturalization" is a more realistic approach than "restoration" to improving aquatic habitats in the YMD, but a systematic approach similar to that outlined by the NRC will greatly improve probabilities of success.

Natural processes that depend on the flood cycle and the forest in flood plain habitats have not existed in the YMD for decades and are not well documented in the YMD. In addition, communities of fish species that were present before major disruption of these processes are not known. Studies from other locations and an understanding of life history patterns of species in the YMD provide a starting point to reconstruct these relationships. A quantitative assessment of existing conditions and fish communities in the YMD also is important. As the assessment proceeds, the results can lead to the development of studies to provide a better understanding of the relationships of individual species and fish communities to the physical habitat and to geomorphic and hydrologic processes. With increased knowledge of the aquatic habitat and the processes that influence its biological community, a framework to design and implement naturalization programs that target specific habitats and fish communities can be developed.

Research in the YMD

The YMD is a unique region. It has been intensively affected by human activities, but processes that affect fish communities and their habitat in the YMD have been poorly investigated. The focus of the few surveys and studies has been on sport fishes (Lucas 1985), large species in oxbow lakes (Miranda and Lucas 2004), assessments of habitat improvement projects (Killgore and others 2008b), or syntheses of museum records of fishes collected over the years in the region (Ross 2001). Two important assessments have been completed for the YMD. The first assessment, by the Yazoo River Basin Team, addresses water quality and land use (YRBT 2000). The second assessment, which includes two reports, describes the development of two indices of biological integrity (IBI) for fish in habitats in the Yazoo River Delta and the oxbow lakes in the YMD (Killgore and others 2008a, Miranda and others 2007). These reports provided a description of the water quality, fish communities in the YMD and, in the case of the development of the IBIs, a preliminary analysis of the effects of physical and chemical factors on fish. Both assessments address two pressing issues facing fish in the YMD—sediment and water quality—and provide a plan of action to address them. A better understanding of the interactions of fish with their habitat and the processes in the YMD that influence fish distribution and abundance is needed to address the larger tasks of recreating natural processes and habitat restoration.

Some of the major processes and habitats that influence fish distribution in the YMD were discussed in earlier sections of this paper. The few studies that describe the response of fish to natural processes have been conducted outside the YMD. These studies can provide a template for naturalization/rehabilitation projects for the YMD. However, systematic and quantitative studies within the YMD are essential to effective and efficient development, implementation, and evaluation of such projects. Three major unanswered questions concerning the fish communities in the YMD are proposed.

1. What are the limiting factors that affect fish abundance and diversity?

2. How do ecological processes and disturbances structure aquatic habitats and fish communities?

3. What are the relationships between fish communities and habitat structure?

No priority is assigned to the three categories. Studies within one category may have application to other questions in other categories. The purpose at this point is to identify an approach and to provide some examples of studies that can begin to address these large and complex questions. The results of these studies can contribute to the development, evaluation, and implementation of projects designed to reestablish natural function of aquatic habitats.

What Are the Limiting Factors That Affect Fish Abundance and Diversity?

One prerequisite to an effective program to improve conditions for fish is to identify characteristics of their habitat that limit their abundance and diversity. These conditions may be physical features of the habitat, such as space and cover, water quality, or the biological characteristics of the desired species. The index of biotic integrity developed by Killgore and others (2008a) for the YMD provides a starting point to identify several variables that may limit populations. Access to critical habitats is linked to isolation of the flood plain by levees or dams and is one example of a limiting factor of fish abundance and diversity. The diversity of species and the range of anthropogenic disturbance in the YMD create a complex environment for limiting factors analysis.

Fish communities respond to water and habitat quality. Killgore and others (2008b) separated species into those tolerant and intolerant of low water quality, and certain species—gars and bowfins—are adapted to survive low dissolved oxygen conditions. Other species require higher concentrations of dissolved oxygen. Establishment of measurable criteria to identify "tolerant" and "intolerant" species along a gradient would provide a useful tool to examine water quality as a limiting factor.

Increased knowledge of life histories of individual species can contribute to understanding the response to effects such as limited access to spawning habitats, seasonal changes in dissolved oxygen, or cumulative effects of sediment accumulation. Often water quality is cited as a limiting factor for fish; however, connectivity among habitats can be important if access to critical habitats is blocked. Three questions within this category provide a starting point for the analysis.

1. Can measures of water quality and habitat quality be used to determine the relative tolerance of species to environmental conditions?

2. What is the effect of seasonal fluxes in dissolved oxygen on fish communities in perennial habitats in the YMD?

3. Does connectivity between riverine and flood plain habitats limit fish species diversity in the YMD?

Studies addressing these questions can form the basis for a limiting factors analysis that systematically evaluates physical and biological conditions that may increase diversity and abundance of target species. Results also may be used to establish regulatory standards such as for total maximum daily loads (TMDL) for potential stressors such as dissolved oxygen. One desirable outcome of the investigation of limiting factors is the development of a model that can be used to prioritize and evaluate potential outcomes of habitat improvement projects.

How Do Ecological Processes and Disturbances Structure Aquatic Habitats and Fish Communities?

Seasonal floods are keystone events in the YMD, but the process is substantially altered from the natural state. Although fish movement onto the flood plain during high water is reasonably well documented, the effect of timing and duration of flooding on the species of the YMD is not well known. Some fish communities may be dependent on seasonal flooding to complete their life histories (obligate); others may be opportunistic users of the flood plain (facultative). The ability to exploit the flood plain can affect fish communities in adjacent habitats. Spawning of many species in the YMD occurs during periods of high water in the late winter and spring. Timing, duration, and water quality may affect spawning success of some species.

Afforestation, the term used to describe planting agricultural land with trees, is used to reestablish commercial forests in the YMD. This practice also offers an opportunity to "naturalize" aquatic habitats located within the newly created forests. A quantitative evaluation of the fish communities and aquatic habitats in agricultural lands, forested lands, and afforested lands would provide a starting point for a systematic approach to a naturalization program for the YMD.

A few questions that address these issues are:

1. Which species are obligate users of the flood pulse and which are facultative users of the flood pulse?

2. How do timing and duration of floods affect water quality and the fish communities on the flood plain?

3. How does the flood pulse affect fish communities on batture land?

4. How do fish communities respond to seasonal floods in forested habitats and habitats in afforested lands?

Water and habitat quality also are linked to connectivity between the flood plain and the river. Water quality variables are likely to respond differently to seasonal floods and influence fish populations. Understanding how fish respond to seasonal floods can contribute to the development of techniques to control water levels in habitats isolated by levees and other flood control structures.

What Are the Relationships between Fish Communities and Habitat Structure?

The development of a method to classify habitats based on measurable geomorphic and hydrological features that can be related to fish/aquatic organisms is an important starting point in the analysis of relationships between fish and habitats. Such a methodology can be used to stratify habitats to determine relationships. It would also provide a useful tool for inventory and assessment of habitat that could be applied during planning of restoration projects.

Complexity within habitats appears to be greatly reduced throughout the YMD. The removal of large riparian trees throughout the YMD and large-scale removal of large wood from nearly all flowing waters have substantially altered the physical habitat in most rivers, streams, and bayous. Furthermore, removal of instream wood has shaped the human perception of habitat complexity. In many areas of the Southeastern United States, large wood has not received the same emphasis as an integral part of fish habitat as it has elsewhere (Bisson and others 1987, Bryant and Sedell 1995). Benke and others (1985) recognized the importance of large wood to aquatic production, and Warren and others (2002) observed correlations between fish abundance and large wood in the loessial region of north central Mississippi. The effects of large wood accumulations on channel morphology and fish in the YMD were recognized by Shields and others (2000). However, the response of fish communities and abundance has not been explored for the YMD.

Some of the questions that begin to address these issues are:

1. How do fish communities differ among major habitat classifications in the YMD?

2. What is the distribution of large wood in the YMD and its effect on species diversity and abundance?

3. How does habitat structure created by large wood and artificial structures such as large rock rip-rap affect fish communities?

4. Do riparian buffer strips increase habitat complexity, and what is their effect on the fish community?

The habitats in the YMD are diverse and range from large rivers to small sloughs and ephemeral ponds. Within each of these habitats, the complexity and structure also vary with corresponding effects on fish communities. Large wood may be a common feature that defines habitat structure in most of them. The preceding questions offer one approach to investigate how habitat structure influences fish communities in the YMD.

The three categories are relatively broad in scope, but provide a means of organizing an approach to understanding processes in aquatic ecosystems of the YMD that affect fish. The questions are examples that address gaps in information needed for projects to improve aquatic habitat quality in the YMD. They also provide a starting point for a larger discussion among agencies and stakeholders to develop a comprehensive research program for the YMD. This program can form a foundation for management of fish and aquatic resources.

Collaboration among government agencies, landowners, and nongovernmental organizations is an essential element in the successful implementation of a research program in the YMD. Collaboration needs to begin with planning and prioritizing a comprehensive long-term program. This process can identify the most critical information needs for ongoing and future restoration and management programs for the YMD. As studies are developed, coordination of effort among groups will contribute to efficient allocation of resources. Cooperative research has the advantage of forming a critical mass to undertake large-scale and long-term studies, whereas independent studies can focus on smaller short-term projects.

The Yazoo River Basin Team organization provides a template to develop a comprehensive and collaborative research agenda for the YMD (YRBT 2000). The team is broad based with representatives from Federal, State, and local government agencies, from stakeholder organizations representing landowners, and from nongovernment organizations such as The Nature Conservancy. The team has developed and implemented a long-range plan for management and restoration of aquatic habitats for the YMD. It provides a forum to coordinate existing projects, to apply new ideas, to propose and discuss new projects, and to generate and maintain public awareness of fish and aquatic resource management. All of these elements are essential for a successful, collaborative research effort that would complement a successful regional restoration and management program.

Summary

The Mississippi River and the LMAV are products of geological processes that have continued since the early Eocene > 50 million years BP. The river has maintained its north-south location on the North American continent for the past 1.2 million years. During this time, the watershed has been exposed to extensive shifts in climate, sea level, and sediment regimes. The presence of ancient fish species, such as gar and bowfin, and the persistence of the large species assemblage in the Mississippi River valley may be attributed to the river's long geological history and north-south orientation. The present diverse fish community of the LMAV developed as a result of its geological and geomorphic history.

The Mississippi River alternated between a braided system and a meandering system through its geological history. Its present meandering phase formed about 9,000 years BP and shaped the present morphology of the YMD. Nearly all aquatic habitats in the YMD were formed as a result of channel meanders across the flood plain. Distributary channels, oxbow lakes, sloughs, bayous, and swamps were formed through the succession of meander bends and cutoffs from abandoned channels. Levees, flood control structures, land use practices, and loss of large wood in stream and river channels have modified and curtailed these processes throughout most of the YMD.

Virtually all of the landscape in the YMD has been modified by human activity. Logging and land clearing for large-scale agriculture have removed nearly all of the hardwood forests in the YMD. Only patches remain, and these are regrowth from previous land clearing. Agriculture has removed most of the natural contours formed by meander scrolls and abandoned stream channels. Streams and bayous have been channelized (straightened) and ditched to facilitate drainage. Loss of riparian trees, in combination with snagging and channel clearing, has removed most large wood from rivers, streams, and bayous throughout the YMD. Levees and flood control structures, including bypass channels, have isolated most of the historic flood plain and have greatly attenuated the formation of new aquatic habitats in the flood plain of the YMD. However, the levees have created a new landscape, the batture land between the levees and the river where new aquatic habitats were created. Large areas of bottomland forest exist in batture land, but few examples of aquatic habitats exist that resemble those found in the YMD before European development either in the batture land or in the YMD flood plain.

As with its landscape, the hydrology of the YMD has been substantially modified from its natural cycle. It is still driven by seasonal climatic events and upstream conditions of rainfall and snowmelt; however, the duration and intensity of the upstream discharge cycle have been altered by upstream human activity. Within the YMD, the flood pulse has been changed both qualitatively and quantitatively. The Mississippi River no longer floods laterally across the flood plain. Connectivity is maintained as floodwaters back up the tributaries that flow across parts of the flood plain not isolated by levees. Drainage is accelerated on agricultural land and prolonged elsewhere by dams. All of these factors removed the natural dynamic flow and ebb of the flood pulse across the flood plain. Although little remains of the natural hydrology of the YMD, fish move in and out of the remaining flood plain on the altered flood pulse.

Most of the larger fish species present during aboriginal occupation of the YMD are still present. Few archeological remains exist for smaller species, such as many of the Cyprinidae and smaller Percidae (darters); therefore, their diversity before development in the YMD is not known. These two families are a diverse group within the YMD, and within these families few species are listed as "species of concern" (Ross 2001). Given the large-scale loss of habitat

throughout the YMD and the deterioration of water quality in much of the remaining habitat, the abundance of most species likely has declined. Fish communities may have changed, but this is difficult to assess based on the historical record. Although the general habitat requirements of most species are known (Ross 2001), the relationships of the fish to specific habitat features and their response to disturbance are not well defined for most species. Furthermore, responses of fish communities to the large-scale alterations of aquatic processes in the YMD are not clear.

In the past few years, management of aquatic habitats in the YMD has centered on mitigating and preventing some of the adverse effects of anthropogenic disturbance, primarily intensive agriculture. Effort has been made to reduce sediment and chemical input to water bodies and to address other easily observable effects, including control of aquatic vegetation. These projects provide obvious benefits; however, a broader approach that restores natural aquatic processes can lead to more permanent and cost-effective measures. The research approach proposed in this paper is a starting point to develop an understanding of the response of fish communities to important processes in the aquatic ecosystem of the YMD. Understanding these relationships can contribute to a sustainable rehabilitation program within the socioeconomic context of the YMD.

Acknowledgments

The technical reviews by Jack Killgore, Ph.D., Doug Shields, Ph.D., and Paul Hamel, Ph.D. were extremely helpful. I thank them for sharing their insights on the Delta from their years of experience working in the region. The discussions with Paul Hamel, Emile Gardiner, and others at the Center for Bottomland Hardwood Research provided invaluable insights and were enjoyable. I learned a great deal from them. I was fortunate to meet Ed Jackson, Ph.D. of the University of Southern Mississippi at his research site in Winterville, MS. He not only shared his knowledge of the early aboriginal cultures and their use of fish but also provided data on the fish remains that he and his team discovered. Don Jackson, Ph.D. shared his perspectives and papers on the importance of fish to the people in the area. I appreciate the support and positive environment created by Ted Leininger, Ph.D. and Mel Warren, Ph.D.

Literature Cited

Amoros C.; Bornette, G. 2002. Connectivity and biocomplexity in waterbodies of riverine floodplains. Freshwater Biology. 47: 761–776.

Arendt, J.D.; Wilson, D.S. 1999. Countergradient selection for rapid growth in pumpkinseed sunfish: disentangling ecological and evolutionary effects. Ecology. 80(8): 2793–2798.

Autin W.J.; Burns, S.F.; Miller, B.J. [and others]. 1991. Quaternary geology of the lower Mississippi Valley. In: Morrison, R.B., ed. Quaternary nonglacial geology: conterminous U.S. Boulder, CO: The Geological Society of America: 547–582.

Baker, J.A.; Killgore, K.J.; Kasul, R.L. 1991. Aquatic habitats and fish communities in the lower Mississippi River. Reviews in Aquatic Sciences. 3(4): 313–356.

Barko, V.A.; Herzog, D.P.; O'Connell, M.T. 2006. Response of fishes to floodplain connectivity during and following a 500-year flood event in the unimpounded upper Mississippi River. Wetlands. 26(1): 244–257.

Barry, J.M. 1998. Rising tide. New York: Simon & Schuster. 524 p.

Benke, A.C.; Henry, R.L.; Gillespie, D.M.; Hunter, D.M. 1985. Importance of snag habitat for animal production in southeastern streams. Fisheries. 10(5): 8–13.

Biedenharn, D.S.; Thorne, C.R.; Watson, C.C. 2000. Recent morphological evolution of the Lower Mississippi River. Geomorphology. 34(3-4): 227–249.

Bisson, P.A.; Bilby, R.E.; Bryant, M.D. [and others]. 1987. Large woody debris in forested streams in the Pacific Northwest: past, present, and future. In: Salo, E.O.; Cundy, T.W., eds. Streamside management: forestry and fishery interactions: Proceedings of a conference. Seattle: University of Washington, Seattle. College of Forest Resources: 143–190.

Boschung, H.T.; Mayden, R.L. 2004. Fishes of Alabama. Washington, DC: Smithsonian Books. 726 p.

Breitburg, E. 1998. Faunal remains. In: Chapman, S.; Walling, R., eds. Archaeological data recovery at the McNight site (22CO560), Coahoma County, Mississippi. Report prepared for the Mississippi Department of Transportation by Pan-American Consultants, Inc. Memphis TN: 209–216. On file at: Southern Hardwoods Laboratory, 432 Stoneville Road, Stoneville, MS 38776.

Briggs, J.C. 1986. Introduction to the zoogeography of North American fishes. In: Hocutt, C.H.; Wiley, E.O., eds. The zoogeography of North American fishes. New York: John Wiley: 1–16.

Brinson, M.M.; Swift, B.L.; Plantico, R.C.; Barclay, J.S. 1981. Riparian ecosystems: their ecology and status. Biological Services Publication FWS/OBS 81/17. Kearneysville, WV: Department of the Interior, U.S. Fish & Wildlife Service. 154 p.

Brown, A.V.; Brown, K.B.; Jackson, D.C.; Pierson, W.K. 2005. Lower Mississippi River and its tributaries. In: Benke, A.C.; Cushing, C.E., eds. Rivers of North America. New York: Elsevier Press: 231–281.

Brown, C.; Fenn, T.; Hinks, S. [and others]. 1994. A cultural resource assessment of the Palusha Creek 2 site, 22LF649, Leflore County, Mississippi. Report prepared for the U.S. Army Corps of Engineers by Christopher Goodwin and Associates, Inc. (New Orleans, LA). New Orleans: [Not paged]. On file at: Southern Hardwoods Laboratory, 432 Stoneville Road, Stoneville, MS 38776.

Bryant, M.D.; Sedell, J.R. 1995. Riparian forests, wood in the water, and fish habitat complexity. In: Armantrout, N.B., ed. Condition of the world's aquatic habitats: Proceedings of the World Fisheries Congress. Athens, Greece: Oxford & IBH Publishing Co.: 202–224.

Capone, T.A.; Kushlan, J.A. 1991. Fish community structure in dry-season stream pools. Ecology. 72(3): 983–992.

Clayton, A.; Knight V.J., Jr.; Moore, E.C., eds. 1993. The DeSoto Chronicles: the expedition of Hernando de Soto to North America in 1539–1543, Volume 1. Tuscaloosa, AL: The University of Alabama Press. 569 p.

Conner, W.H.; Sharitz, R.R. 2005. Forest communities of bottomlands. In: Fredrickson, L.H., King, S.L.; Kaminski, R.M., eds. Ecology and management of bottomland hardwood systems: the state of our understanding. Special Publication No. 10. Puxico, MO: University of Missouri-Columbia. Gaylord Memorial Laboratory: 93–120.

Coxe, C.L. 1999. Vertebrate faunal analysis. In: Perrault, S.L.; Davoli, E.L.; Coxe, C.L.; Cash, W., eds. Cultural resources inventory, Upper Steele Bayou project, Swan Lake mitigation area, Washington County, Mississippi. Report prepared for the U.S. Army Corps of Engineers by Coastal Environments, Inc. (Baton Rouge, LA). Vicksburg, MS: 225–232. On file at: Southern Hardwoods Laboratory, 432 Stoneville Road, Stoneville, MS 38776.

Cross, F.B.; Mayden, R.L.; Stewart, J.D. 1986. Fishes in the western Mississippi basin (Missouri, Arkansas and Red Rivers). In: Hocutt, C.H.; Wiley, E.O., eds. The zoogeography of North American freshwater fishes. New York: John Wiley: 363–412.

Crossman, E.J.; McAllister, D.E. 1986. Zoogeography of freshwater fishes of the Hudson Bay drainage, Ugava Bay and Arctic Archipelago. In: Hocutt, C.H.; Wiley, E.O., eds. The zoogeography of North American freshwater fishes. New York: John Wiley: 53–104.

Delcourt, H. 1987. The impact of prehistoric agriculture and land occupation on natural vegetation. Trends in Ecology & Evolution. 2(2): 39–44.

Delcourt, P.A.; Delcourt, H.R. 1987. Long-term forest dynamics of the temperate zone: a case study of late-quaternary forests in eastern North America. New York: Springer-Verlag. 439 p.

Delcourt, P.A.; Delcourt, H.R.; Morse, D.F.; Morse, P.A. 1993. History, evolution, and organization of vegetation and human culture. In: Martin, W.H.; Boyce, S.G.; Echternacht, A.C., eds. Biodiversity of the Southeastern United States: lowland terrestrial communities. New York: John Wiley: 47–49.

Ewing, M.S. 1991. Turbidity control and fisheries enhancement in a bottomland hardwood backwater system in Louisiana (U.S.A.). Regulated Rivers: Research & Management 6(2): 87–99.

Finger, T.R.; Stewart, E.M. 1987. Response of fishes to flooding regime in lowland hardwood wetlands. In: Matthews, W.J.; Heins, D.C., eds. Community and evolutionary ecology of North American stream fishes. Norman, OK: University of Oklahoma Press: 86–92.

Fisk, H.N. 1944. Geological investigation of the alluvial valley of the lower Mississippi valley. Vicksburg, MS: U.S. Army Corps of Engineers, Mississippi River Commission. 78 p.

Franklin, S.B.; Wasklewicz, T.; Grubaugh, J.W.; Greulich, S. 2003. Hydrologic stage periodicity of the Mississippi River before and after systematic channel modifications. Journal of the American Water Resources Association. 39(3): 637–648.

Galat, D.L.; Fredrickson, L.H.; Humburg, D.D. [and others]. 1998. Flooding to restore connectivity of regulated, large-river wetlands. BioScience. 48: 721–733.

Goulding, M. 1980. The fishes and the forest: explorations in Amazonian natural history. Berkeley, CA: University of California Press. 280 p.

Guillory, V. 1979. Utilization of an inundated floodplain by Mississippi River fishes. Florida Scientist. 42(4): 222–228.

Gutreuter, S.; Bartels, A.D.; Irons, K.; Sandheinrich, M.B. 1999. Evaluation of the flood-pulse concept based on statistical models of growth of selected fishes of the Upper Mississippi River system. Canadian Journal of Fisheries and Aquatic Sciences. 56(12): 2282.

Halupka, K.C.; Willson, M.F.; Bryant, M.D. [and others]. 2003. Conservation of population diversity of Pacific salmon in southeast Alaska. North American Journal of Fisheries Management. 23(4): 1057–1086.

Hamel, P.; Buckner, E.R. 1998. How far could a squirrel travel in the treetops? a prehistory of the southern forest. In: Transactions of the 63rd North American Wildlife and Natural Resources Conference. Washington, DC: Wildlife Management Institute: 309–315.

Harper, R M. 1912. Botanical evidence of the age of certain ox-bow lakes. Science. 36(935): 760–761.

Hilborn, R.; Quinn, T.P.; Schindler, D.E.; Rogers, D.E. 2003. Biocomplexity and fisheries sustainability. Proceedings of the National Academy of Sciences. Washington, DC: National Academy of Sciences. 100(11): 6564–6568.

Hodges, J.D. 1994. The southern bottomland hardwood region and brown loam bluffs subregion. In: Barret, J.W., ed. Regional Silviculture of the United States. New York: John Wiley: 227–269.

Holland, L.E.; Bryan, C.F.; Newman, J.P. 1983. Water quality and the rotifer population in the Atchafalaya River basin, Louisiana. Hydrobiologia. 98(1): 55–69.

Hooke, J.M. 2004. Cutoffs galore! occurrence and causes of multiple cutoffs on a meandering river. Geomorphology. 61(3–4): 225–228.

Hoover J.J.; Killgore, K.J. 1998. Fish communities. In: Messina, M.G.; Conner, W.H., eds. Southern forested wetlands: ecology and management. Boca Raton, LA: Lewis Publishers: 237–260.

Hoover, J.J.; Killgore, K.J. 2002. Small floodplain pools as habitat for fishes and amphibians: methods for evaluation. ERDC TN EMRRP EM 03. Vicksburg, MS: U.S. Army Engineer Research and Development Center. 13 p.

Howard, R.J.; Allen, J.A. 1989. Streamside habitats in southern forested wetlands: their role and implications for management. In: Hook, D.D.; Lea, R., eds. Proceedings of the symposium: The forested wetlands of the Southern United States. Gen. Tech. Rep. SE–50. Asheville, NC: U.S. Department of Agriculture Forest Service, Southeastern Forest Experiment Station: 97–106.

Hudson, C. 1997. Knights of Spain, warriors of the sun: Hernando de Soto and the South's ancient chiefdoms. Athens, GA: University of Georgia Press. 561 p.

Hudson, P.F.; Kesel, R.H. 2000. Channel migration and meander-bend curvature in the lower Mississippi River prior to major human modification. Geology. 28(6): 531–534.

Hupp, C.R.; Walbridge, M.R.; Lockaby, B.G. 2005. Fluvial geomorphic processes and landforms, water quality, and nutrients in bottomland hardwood forests of southeastern USA. In: Fredrickson, L.H.; King, S.L.; Kaminski, R.M., eds. Ecology and management of bottomland hardwood systems: the state of our understanding. Special Publication No. 10. Puxico, MO: University of Missouri-Columbia. Gaylord Memorial Laboratory: 37–55.

Jackson, D.A.; Mandrak, N.E. 2002. Changing fish biodiversity: predicting the loss of cyprinid biodiversity due to global climate change. In: McGinn, N.A., ed. Fisheries in a changing climate. American Fisheries Society Symposium 32, Bethesda, MD: American Fisheries Society: 89–98.

Jackson, D.C. 2004. Fisheries dynamics in the Yazoo River Basin. In: Welcomme, R.L.; Petr, T., eds. Proceedings of the second international symposium on the management of large rivers for fisheries: volume 2. RAP Publication 2004/17. Bangkok: FAO Regional Office for Asia and the Pacific: 103–115.

Jackson, D.C. 2005. Fisheries dynamics in temperate floodplain rivers. In: Fredrickson, L.H.; King, S.L.; Kaminski, R.M., eds. Ecology and management of bottomland hardwood systems: the state of our understanding. Special Publication No. 10. Puxico, MO: University of Missouri-Columbia, Gaylord Memorial Laboratory: 201–212.

Jackson, D.C.; Francis, J.M.; Ye, Q. 1997. Hand grappling blue catfish in the main channel of a Mississippi river. North American Journal of Fisheries Management. 17: 1019–1024.

Jackson, D.C.; Ye, Q. 2000. Riverine fish stock and regional agronomic responses to hydrological and climatic regimes in the upper Yazoo River basin. Cowx, I.G., ed. Management and ecology of river fisheries. Oxford, UK: Fishing News Books: 242–257.

Junk, W.G.; Bayley, P.B.; Sparks, R.E. 1989. The flood pulse concept in river-floodplain systems. Canadian Special Publications of Fisheries and Aquatic Sciences. 106: 110–127.

Kaeser, A.J.; Litts, T.L. 2008. An assessment of deadhead logs and large woody debris using side scan sonar and field surveys in streams of southwest Georgia. Fisheries. 33(12): 589–597.

Kemper, J.P. 1928. Floods in the valley of the Mississippi. New Orleans: National Flood Commission. 255 p.

Killgore, K.J.; Baker, J.A. 1996. Patterns of larval fish abundance in a bottomland hardwood wetland. Wetlands. 16: 288–295.

Killgore, K.J.; Hoover, J.J. 1992. A guild for monitoring and evaluating fish communities in bottomland hardwood wetlands. WRP Technical Note FW-EV-2.2. Vicksburg, MS: U.S. Army Engineer Research and Development Center. 7 p.

Killgore, K.J.; Hoover, J.; Murphy, C.; George, S. 2008a. Index of biological integrity for fishes of the Yazoo River Delta, Mississippi (draft). Vicksburg, MS: U.S. Army Corps of Engineers, Engineer Research and Development Center. 34 p.

Killgore, K.J.; Hoover, J.J.; Murphy, C.E. [and others]. 2008b. Restoration of delta streams: a case history and conceptual model. EMRRP Technical Notes Collection. ERDC TN-EMRRP-ER-08. Vicksburg, MS: U.S. Army Engineer Research and Development Center. 19 p.

Kwak, T.J. 1988. Lateral movement and use of floodplain habitat by fishes of the Kankakee River, Illinois. American Midland Naturalist. 120(2): 241-249.

Lucas, G.M. 1985. Survey of the fisheries of the Mississippi Delta. Mississippi Project F-68. Oxford, MS: Mississippi Department of Wildlife Conservation. 51 p.

Maser, C.; Sedell, J.R. 1994. From the forest to the sea: the ecology of wood in streams, rivers, estuaries, and oceans. Delray Beach, FL: St. Lucie Press. 200 p.

Matthews, W.J. 1987. Physicochemical tolerance and selectivity of stream fishes as related to their geographic ranges and local distributions. In: Matthews, W.J.; Heins, D.C., eds. Community and evolutionary ecology of North American stream fishes. Norman, OK: University of Oklahoma Press: 111–120.

Mayden, R.L. 1988. Vicariance biogeography, parsimony, and evolution in North American freshwater fishes. Systematic Zoology. 37(4): 329–355.

Meador, M.R.; Coles, J.F.; Zappia, H. 2005. Fish assemblage responses to urban intensity gradients in contrasting metropolitan areas: Birmingham, Alabama and Boston, Massachusetts. American Fisheries Society Symposium. 47: 409–423.

Miller, R.R. 1965. Quaternary freshwater fishes of North America. In: Wright, H.E., Jr.; Frey, D.G., eds. The quaternary of the United States. Princeton, NJ: Princeton University Press: 569–581.

Miranda, L.E. 2005. Fish assemblages in oxbow lakes relative to connectivity with the Mississippi River. Transactions of the American Fisheries Society. 134: 1480–1489.

Miranda, L.E.; Aycock, J.N.; Miyazono, S.; Steffen, C.J. 2007. Biotic integrity of alluvial lakes in the Yazoo River Basin. Progress Report to U.S. Army Corps of Engineer, Engineer Research and Development Center, Waterways Experiment Station. Starkville, MS: USGS Mississippi Cooperative Fish and Wildlife Unit and Department of Wildlife and Fisheries, Mississippi State University. 47 p.

Miranda, L.E.; Lucas, G.M. 2004. Determinism in fish assemblages of floodplain lakes of the vastly disturbed Mississippi Alluvial Valley. Transactions of the American Fisheries Society. 133: 358–370.

Mooney, J.P.; Wilkerson, S.; Mead, T.; Wilson, J.P. 2003. Cultural resource phase III mitigation of sites 22CO573/773and 22CO788 for the construction of the Coahoma welcome center at the interchange of U.S. Highway 49 and 61. Report prepared for the Mississippi Department of Transportation by Michael Baker, Inc. White Hall, AR. [Not paged]. On file at: Southern Hardwoods Laboratory, 432 Stoneville Road, Stoneville, MS 38776.

National Research Council. 1992. Restoration of aquatic ecosystems. Washington, DC: National Academy Press. 552 p.

Peacock, E.; Haag, W.R.; Warren, M.L. 2004. Prehistoric decline in freshwater mussels coincident with the advent of maize agriculture. Conservation Biology. 19(2): 547–551.

Platt, S.G.; Brantley, C.G. 1997. Canebrakes: an ecological and historical perspective. Castanea. 62(1): 8–21.

Powers, S.L.; Warren, M.L., Jr. 2009. Phylogeography of three snubnose darters (Percidae: subgenus Ulocentra) endemic to the Southeastern U.S. coastal plain. Copeia. 3: 526–531.

Puth, L.M.; Wilson, K.A. 2001. Boundaries and corridors as a continuum of ecological flow control: lessons from rivers and streams. Conservation Biology. 15(1): 21–30.

Putnam, J.A.; Furnival, G M.; McKnight, J.S. 1960. Management and inventory of southern hardwoods. Agric. Handb. 181. Washington, DC: U.S. Department of Agriculture. 102 p.

Rempel, L.L.; Smith, D.G. 1997. Postglacial fish dispersal from the Mississippi refuge to the Mackenzie basin. Canadian Journal of Fisheries and Aquatic Sciences. 55: 893–899.

Richie, J.C.; Cooper, C.M.; McHenry, J.R.; Schiebe, F.R. 1983. Sediment accumulation in Lake Chicot, Arkansas. Environmental Geology. 5(2): 79–82.

Robison, H.W. 1986. Zoogeographic implications of the Mississippi River basin. In: Hocutt, C.H.; Wiley, E.O., eds. The zoogeography of North American freshwater fishes. New York: John Wiley: 267–286.

Ross, S.T. 2001. Inland fishes of Mississippi. Jackson, MS: University Press of Mississippi. 624 p.

Ross, S.T.; Baker, J.A. 1983. The response of fishes to periodic spring floods in a southeastern stream. American Midland Naturalist. 109: 1–14.

Rutherford, D.A.; Gelwicks, K.R.; Kelso, W.E. 2001. Physiochemical effects of the flood pulse in the Atchafalaya River Basin, Louisiana. Transactions of the American Fisheries Society. 130: 276–288.

Saikku, M. 2005. This delta, this land: an environmental history of the Yazoo-Mississippi floodplain. Athens, GA: The University of Georgia Press. 373 p.

Saucier, R.T. 1994. Geomorphology and quaternary geologic history of the lower Mississippi valley. Vicksburg, MS: U.S. Army Engineer Waterways Experiment Station, Mississippi River Commission. 364 p.

Schramm, H.L., Jr.; Eggleton, M.A. 2006. Applicability of the flood-pulse concept in a temperate floodplain river ecosystem: thermal and temporal components. River Research and Applications. 22(5): 543–553.

Schade, C.B.; Bonar, S.A. 2005. Distribution and abundance of nonnative fishes in streams of the western United States. North American Journal of Fisheries Management. 25: 1386–1394.

Scott S.L. 1995. Vertebrate faunal remains. In: Weinstein, R.A.; Fuller, S.; Scott, S.L. [and others]. The rock levee site: late Marksville through late Mississippi period settlement, Boliver County, Mississippi. Report prepared for the U.S. Army Corps of Engineers by Coastal Environments, Inc. (Baton Rouge, LA). Vicksburg, MS: 243–262. On file at: Southern Hardwoods Laboratory, 432 Stoneville Road, Stoneville, MS 38776.

Shankman, D. 1991. Forest regeneration on abandoned meanders of a coastal plain river in western Tennessee. Castanea. 3(56): 157–167.

Sheaffer, W.A.; Nickum, J.G. 1986. Backwater areas as nursery habitats for fishes in pool 13 of the Upper Mississippi River. Hydrobiologia. 136: 131–139.

Shields, F.D., Jr. 2008. Effects of a regional channel stabilization project on suspended sediment yield. Journal of Soil and Water Conservation. 63(2): 59–69.

Shields, F.D.; Knight, S.S.; Cooper, C M. 2000. Cyclic perturbation of lowland river channels and ecological response. Regulated Rivers: Research & Management. 16(4): 307–325.

Shields, F.D.; Knight, S.S; Lizotte, R.E. [N.d.]. General design criteria for river backwater restoration. Oxford, MS: U.S. Department of Agriculture, ARS National Sedimentation Laboratory, Water Quality & Ecology Unit. 25 p.

Skelly, D.; Joseph, L.N.; Possingham, H.P. [and others]. 2007. Evolutionary responses to climate change. Conservation Biology. 21(5): 1353–1355.

Smale, M.A.; Rabeni, C.F. 1995. Hypoxia and hyperthermia tolerances of headwater stream fishes. Transactions of the American Fisheries Society. 124: 698–710.

Smith, G.R. 1981. Late Cenozoic freshwater fishes of North America. Annual Review of Ecology and Systematics. 12: 163–193.

Snedden, G.A.; Kelso, W.E.; Rutherford, D.A. 1999. Diel and seasonal patterns of spotted gar movement and habitat use in the Lower Atchafalaya River basin, Louisiana. Transactions of the American Fisheries Society. 128: 144–154.

Sparks, R.E.; Nelson, J.C.; Yin, Y. 1998. Naturalization of the flood regime in regulated rivers. BioScience. 48(9): 706–720.

Stanturf, J.A.; Goodrick, S.L.; Outcalt, K.W. 2007. Disturbance and coastal forests: a strategic approach to forest management in hurricane impact zones. Forest Ecology and Management. 250: 119–135.

Stanturf, J.A.; Schoenholtz, S.H. 1998. Soils and landforms. In: Messina, M.G.; Conner, W.H., eds. Southern forested wetlands: ecology and management. Boca Raton, LA: Lewis Publishers: 123–147.

Thomaz, S M.; Bini, L.M.; Bozelli, R.L. 2007. Floods increase similarity among aquatic habitats in river-floodplain systems. Hydrobiologia. 579(1): 1–13.

Tockner, K.; Pennetzdorfer, D.; Reiner, F.; Ward, J. V. 1999. Hydrological connectivity, and the exchange of organic matter and nutrients in a dynamic river-floodplain system (Danube, Austria). Freshwater Biology. 41(3): 521–535.

Turner, T.F.; Trexler, J.C.; Miller, G.L.; Toyer, K.E. 1994. Temporal and spatial dynamics of larval and juvenile fish abundance in a temperate floodplain river. Copeia. 1: 174–183.

Wallace, J.B.; Benke, A.C. 1984. Quantification of wood habitat in subtropical coastal plain streams. Canadian Journal of Fisheries and Aquatic Sciences. 41(11): 1643–1652.

Warren, M.L.; Burr, B.M.; Walsh, S.J. [and others]. 2000. Diversity, distribution, and conservation status of the freshwater fishes of the Southern United States. Fisheries. 25(10): 7–29.

Warren, M.L.; Haag, W.R.; Wendell, R.; Adams, S.B. 2002. Forest linkages to diversity and abundance in lowland stream fish communities. In: Holland, M M.; Warren, M.L.; Stanturf, J.A., eds. Proceedings of a conference on sustainability of wetlands and water resources. Gen. Tech. Rep. SRS–50. Asheville, NC: U.S. Department of Agriculture Forest Service, Southern Research Station: 168–182.

Wilson R.C. 1987. Analysis of the faunal remains from the French Site 22Ho565/19 p10, Holmes County, Mississippi. In: Marshall, R. A. ed. Archaeological data recovery at the French Site. Cobb Institute of Archaeology, Mississippi State University, Starkville: 1-10.

Yazoo River Basin Team (YRBT). 2000. Yazoo River Basin Status Report 2000. Jackson, MS: Mississippi Department of Environmental Quality. 29 p. http://www.deq.state.ms.us. [Date accessed: March 2009].